The

Façade

By Channel N. Walker

Copyright © 2013 Channel Walker

CHANNEL WALKER

All rights reserved. No parts of this book may be reproduced in any form or by any means without written permission from the author, except in brief quotes to be used in reviews.
ISBN:9781493593538
ISBN-13:9781493593538

Acknowledgments

I would like to take this time and say thank you to all my friends who supported me through this journey. It wasn't easy but you guys stood beside me and gave me encouraging words and to that I say thank you.

Special thank you to the two most important women in my life, Waleada Brown and LaQuandra Charlton. I appreciate you two because you two put in the time, the effort and listened to my constant questions without any complaints and kept your faith in me. Each of you played a different role but through it all you both kept me reaching my goal telling me to block out the negative energy and rechanneling it with the positive. I love you both unconditionally. I can't say thank you enough.

Lataryn Rainey-Perry Thank you Thank you Thank you beyond words can say. Your truly an amazing person and Im so happy I met you, thank you again for your support and your dedication to helping me prosper as a better writer. Thank you again.

THE FACADE

Facade - (n) an outward appearance that is maintained to conceal a less pleasant or creditable reality.

Prologue

"PLEASE I CANT BREATH!" I screamed as the lighter and pipe I held in my hands fell to the floor. I was just about to inhale the white smoke that had begun to fill it, when I felt a pair of rough hands grip my neck and start to squeeze the life out of me. I scratched and clawed at the hands of this unknown person as my eyes frantically darted around the room in hopes of spotting something I could use to fight back with. There was nothing in sight. I fought to breathe as I felt my body gravitating towards the dirty shower in the bathroom that I was in. I had come there to feed my craving and was expecting to be floating on cloud nine soon after, but instead I was in here fighting for my life and I had no clue who the hands gripping my neck belonged to. I feel myself becoming light headed and all I could think about was how I'm here in this dirty broke down abandoned house that might possibly become my grave soon. Is this how I'm going to die? Did Thomas sell me out and was trying to get rid of me? Questions were flooding my mind as I struggled to breathe. Even in this fucked up situation I wished that I was able to at least get my high before I died, that way I wouldn't feel a thing. My eyes suddenly felt heavier and it was becoming harder and harder to keep them open. Then out of nowhere something went SNAP!

    I fell into the tub with a big bang hitting my back against the soap holder built into the wall. I screamed in agony! I can't help myself and nobody can hear me. I stop screaming, I feel myself nodding off, my eyes are still heavy but I see a figure standing over me, it was Thomas. I struggled to keep my eyes open and saw another figure approaching . Before I could form my lips to speak darkness consumed me.

Gregg

The disgust I feel when she is in my presence goes beyond words. It would've been so easy for me to walk away, but for the sake of my family and commitment to my vows— I'm still here hating life. *SHE*, my wife, is a woman I despise. Sitting in my butter soft leather reclining chair with a shot of Hennessey on the rocks and the Providence Journal, I sensed her presence in the kitchen. She was preparing dinner—we hardly acknowledge each other these days. From the corner of the paper I could see her back facing me, in a white tank top and some gray slacks, humming and acting so care free. I get a glimpse of her wedding ring shimmering. I would prefer her to take it off, so I don't have a constant reminder that the woman I married isn't the poise and humble woman everyone thinks she is.

When Isaiah was first born her preparing dinner was such a turn on. I felt like the luckiest man in the world. I would take her from behind pressing her up against the cutting board and grab her by her thick mane and we would have great sex in the kitchen. That's how Elijah was created. My wife and I had such a fire that burned between us and I couldn't get enough of her. She made me feel so young and alive.

Interrupting my thoughts, I hear my princess Naomi calling my name.

"Hey daddy!"

I see Gail look at us for a moment and we catch each other's eye. She rolls her eyes and I turn my attention back to my baby girl. Staring into my little lady's honey brown eyes, I smile and recall the days of watching her grow from being a small little baby to a gorgeous little girl. I could recall the day she was born as if it were yesterday. When the doctor laid her in my arms, her honey brown eyes looking up at me and she gave me a smile, from that moment on she was daddy's little girl and the love I have for my little princess was indescribable.

"Tanya is having a slumber party and she invited me." She smiled and handed me the pink flowered invitation. "I really wanna go."

She batted her bambi-like eyes and pouted innocently. I just smiled and listened.

"Oh yeah and when we have our day out on Saturday, can we take a trip to the mall and get her a gift daddy?"

Overlooking the invitation I reply "Sure baby girl."

"Thanks daddy, you're the best." She jumped up onto my lap and hugged my neck tightly.

"Sorry to break up this little moment, but miss Naomi you have chores to do in this house before you make any ongoing plans for the weekend. Your homework needs to be done, let's not forget our responsibilities in this house before any slumber party." Gail said and shoots me a look of disgust.

I stare at her just as hard back, wondering who she thinks she is. Some days I wonder if she is jealous of me and my daughter's relationship. Well at least that's the way it comes off. Naomi huffed and pouts again, then turns and slowly begin to walk away with her head hung low.

Gail stopped her in her tracks and says. "Young lady you better fix your face now."

Naomi looks over at me with eyes begging for me to not let her mother ruin her slumber party plans. As always, I come to my baby girl's defense.

"Gail, lighten up. I'm sure she did her homework at the after school program. Don't ruin the child's fun with your bitter attitude."

Gail fold her arms over her breast and glare at me. "Well Gregg in this family, I will not allow any children of mine to be disrespectful to me and get away with it!" She then walked towards me and I stand up. Her breast were against my chest, that's the most we've touched in months.

"Why must you come up in here with your dark cloud hovering over your head and ruin everyone else's day? You treat your daughter as if she's competition or something."

Gail's face turned red and her eyes become dark as she comments back "And what exactly is that supposed to mean my *perfect* husband? Are you insinuating that I'm jealous of my child?"

"I'm saying you're tripping and you need to calm down. Half the time I don't even know who you are anymore, you've changed and I can't say it's been for the better."

"Hmm let's see. I put my life on hold, gave you three kids and spent the last 15 years of my life being married to your ungrateful ass. So, yeah you damn right I've changed. Unfortunately I can't say the same for you because you're still the boring ass banker that I met 15 years ago."

I smiled inside, I knew I could get under her skin. Doing that always allows me to see her real emotions, instead of the fake persona she puts up all the damn time. I was over this argument and her, so I decided to walk off instead of responding. As I walk off I feel something hard hit me in my back. I swiftly turn on my heels to see the table lamp broken into pieces on the floor. Suddenly something came over me and I rush over to Gail. I was so close to her that I could taste her disgusting breath.

Looking her square in the eyes I say. "Luckily for you our children are watching us. I suggest you go and clean yourself up. You're foaming at the mouth."

She had no idea that Isaiah and Elijah had come to watch her fiasco. I looked over at Isaiah, who is hugging Naomi as she sobs into his chest, and Elijah just watching. I head straight for the front door, once outside I take a couple deep breaths and count to ten trying to calm myself down. I pull my phone from my pocket and call my brother Thomas.

"Hello?... yea bro um, can you meet me somewhere?...I need a break from this house and a stiff drink."

Thomas was two years younger than me, but we looked just alike except he was lighter toned with honey brown eyes like Naomi. He has a medium build with a Cesar haircut and a beard that the ladies love. Thomas always knew how to charm the panties off women. It was because of him that I met Gail.

Right after one of those URI parties, we bumped into her and he hooked us up. I knew she was the one from the moment I met her. I really missed those days. I can't blame him for Gail's indiscretions, but man this lady isn't right. Thomas agreed to meet me at South Street bar and lounge. I jumped into my Nissan Venza and headed to South Providence.

Thomas

When my brother called, I knew he needed to talk I could hear the stress in his voice. Recently he and Gail had been having some marital issues and a lot more tension was rising with suspicions of her infidelities. I sat in my Avalon waiting for Gregg to pull into South Street. I decided I would roll a woo banger real quick before he got there, so I broke my weed up into an old receipt paper. Then reached into my glove compartment for my secret stash and added a few broken crack pieces. I sliced the vanilla Dutch with a razor blade that I kept in my mouth and added the contents of the blunt inside the Dutch leaf. I rolled it up real tight and turned the heat on full blast as I twirled my blunt in my fingertips to make sure all the extra particles hanging on, blew off. Turning the heat back off, I skimmed through my music until I found my song

I like to smoke to by Beanie Sigel ft. Jay Z "It's on" and fired up.

Gregg didn't know about my chosen occupation nor did he have a clue that I ran a drug trade from Prairie Avenue to Lockwood Plaza. I took a draw of my woo banger and reclined my chair back closing my eyes. The high was starting to kick in and I felt good this was my escape from all the fucked up shit in this world. I opened my eyes just in time to see Gregg pulling into a parking spot. I quickly sat upright and put the blunt out and start spraying the can of air freshener kept in my whip. I off the little particles of the weed from my jeans onto the floor, popped a piece of spearmint gum into my mouth and exit my ride. Gregg was walking up towards me just as I was locking the doors. We exchange daps and a brotherly hug.

"What's going on bruh?"

"Nothing man trying to stay afloat."

"Yea I see you bruh. You're a pretty motherfucker showing out in your Gucci T-shirt and True Religion Jeans, like we aren't grown men out here."

Greg nods and laughs. "I may be an old cat but my manhood still works like I'm back in high school, so I ain't complaining."

We both just laugh and head inside of South Street. When we entered the bar all eyes were on Gregg and I. We were well respected in the area because of our father. You could feel the shift of energy from the time Gregg and I walked in. The women were trying to catch our attention and the waitresses did all they can to make sure we were taken care of. One waitress was walking by carrying a handful of dirty dishes and staring Gregg down. Just as she threw him a flirtatious smile she bumped into another customer and dropped everything that was in her hands. Gregg and I laughed our asses off as a few of the other customers ran to her aid.

We were sitting in our usual spot in the far back corner of the bar. I called one of the waitresses over so I can place my drink order. The one that came to take my order looked vaguely familiar, but I couldn't put my finger on where I knew her from. I ordered Hennessey on the rocks and Gregg ordered a round of 1738 straight up. I shot him a look.

He raised his brows and says, "Aye, I'm stressed don't judge me."

"Talk to me my bro. What's got you stressing?"

Gregg just shook his head and stares off at nothing.

I nudged him. You good bro?"

He looked at me and I noticed the lines in his forehead were popping out, that's how I know he's thinking.

"Gail." He sighs out of frustration. "I think Gail is having an affair and I noticed that some of our money is disappearing out of our accounts. I haven't confronted her about my suspicions yet, but I plan to. I've also noticed that she is starting to lose a lot weight and isn't attending to her family like she used to."

"No way not Gail, I could never picture her doing that to you man. She loves you and just doesn't seem like the type."

"I never knew there was a specific look for a person who cheats." Gregg shook his head. "If there is one then I'm sure Gail's ass would fit the description perfectly."

I just nod and say. "That is true, you have a point."

He sighs again "Man, she receives texts messages and phone calls all hours of the night and I hear her whispering when she thinks I'm asleep. The money that's been going missing is the money from our business account and I've contacted the bank to get recent transactions mailed to me, so they should be here within the next couple of days."

The lines in Gregg's forehead started to show again and his cheeks were sucked in from him clenching his teeth together. I wave over the bartender and she approaches with a smile distracting me with her bouncing breasts. It was kind of hard not to notice them when they were pretty much busting out of her bra.

"Can I get you gentleman another round?"

"What are we having?" I asked Gregg, then looked at her and saw her staring back at me with a sly grin— like she was undressing me with her eyes.

I cleared my throat "Yeah let me get another Hennessey on the rocks." I looked at Gregg. "You want anything?"

"Yeah I'll take another 1738 straight up."

"Followed by your phone number." I grinned causing her to blush. She had nice butterscotch complexion with brown and blonde hair neatly placed in a bun on top of her head. She wore red lip stick that showed off her plump lips and an all-black shorts outfit that hugged her body and ass just right. She smiled and walked off switching her butt from left to right, she knew I was watching.

"You ok Gregg?" I asked after noticing how quiet he was.

"Yea man I'm good. I was just thinking about dad and how he would've went into his *'son I told you so'* speeches if he were alive. He knew from the moment I brought her home she wasn't good for me, but I didn't listen."

"Gregg don't beat yourself up, you don't own her mistakes only she can be held accountable."

The waitress came back over and placed down two coasters, then she placed our drinks right in front of us. She slid a napkin over to me with her name and number scribbled in black marker that read: *Kim 401-327-6543* ☺.

I give her a smile and she winked at me before walking away. I'm sure she thought my smile meant that I would be hitting her up, but the truth was I had no intentions of calling her. At least no time soon anyway. I just liked the fact that I could get anyone I please, when I please. I did plan to hold on to her number though, she might come in handy for something. I looked over at Gregg and saw him knocking back his shots, so I removed my straw from my glass and threw mines back as well.

I pushed him on the shoulder, "You taking them shots back like a champ bro, I ain't seen you do that in a long time."

He smiled. "Those were my wild days man, but now it helps to ease the frustration and checkout from reality." He then shook his head and clenched his jaw again. "If she is… if I find out that she's been cheating T, I will probably kill her. I don't know how I would be able to tell my kids. I mean how do you explain to your kids that their mom destroyed our family?"

Just as I was thinking of something sound to say that would help him feel a little bit of peace, I started feeling dizzy. Everything around me was becoming blurry and I was feeling woozy. I could still hear Gregg talking ,but his words echoed.

"Thomas? You okay man?"

I felt myself nod weakly before my body slide off the chair and hit the floor hard. Gregg was standings over me calling out for help while people ran over to see what was going on. Someone screamed out *"call 9-1-1."*

The last thing I remembered was feeling like my body was floating towards the car and hearing Gregg telling me to hold on, before I fell into a deep sleep.

Gail

After the argument with Gregg, I was highly pissed off and ready to walk out on this family—myself nor my heart wasn't in it anymore. I wiped my hand over my mouth before I turned around and realized my kids were still watching me. I didn't bring up the argument with their dad

"Naomi you can stop crying now, your dad isn't here to save you, so go set the table for dinner."

She rolls her eyes at me and walks off with an attitude.

"You better check that attitude little girl or we will be having a serious problem up in here." Sometimes I couldn't stand her little smart ass. Gregg spoils her rotten and it just makes me sick, in fact all of them do. Because of Gregg these kids think they can say and do whatever they want around here, they see the way he talks to me and feel like they don't have to respect me either.

"Little bastards." I cursed under my breath and call out to my sons. "Isaiah and Elijah go get washed up for dinner."

Once I heard them moving about, I headed upstairs to the bathroom in the hallway to clean up also. I turned on the hot and cold water and bent over the sink to splash water over my face. I reached for the towel to my right and dry my face and hands. I frowned at my reflection in the mirror. My hair had split ends and my eyes had black rings around them. My clothes were falling off of me and I no longer had the glowing mom look. I had the your turning into a drug addict look and that made me wonder if Gregg had noticed my change in appearance. If he has he sure didn't say anything. I take my hands out my hair and just rest them against the sink.

I used to love my family and my husband—but if my mother would of told me that raising a family took a lot of dedication and hard work, I wouldn't of signed up for the job. This house, these kids and my husband stresses me out. There was a point where I used to feel so lucky to have all of this. But what's so lucky about it now, when you're happier sleeping in an abandoned building after lighting up a crack pipe? I would feel so good and high that some nights I didn't care to even come home. I used to feel so special waking up in a house and having that marriage that most girls dreamed of. But today I'm ready to leave it behind and forget my kids and their existence in this world. I would do anything just to go back to the project days.

Back then you could never miss anything. Fights, parties, arguments, gossip and even death. You name it everyone knew about it and the news travelled from the kids to the adults. There was no such thing as secrets during that those times. I missed my old girlfriend Simone, we used to be adjoined at the hip. People would never see one of us without the other, and if they did then they would know that the other wasn't too far behind.

This private life that I live now is horrible, I hate it and I wanted out.

"Mom" Isaiah knocked "Are you coming to dinner?"

I sigh. I hated being called mom it drove me insane. "Give me five minutes." I called out to him as I stared at the door. The more time I spend in this house the more I feel like there is no need for to continue being a part of this family. I've done my share of dishes laundry and raising kids. I'm ready for me to finally live and I'm tired of pretending. Gregg would be just fine raising these kids without me.

I looked at myself in the mirror once more and shook my head before walking out of the bathroom. I headed back downstairs entering the dining room to see the kids already served themselves. Gregg still hadn't made it back home yet and I didn't feel up to sitting at the table nor did I have an appetite.

"Mom are you going to eat? Can I fix you a plate?" asked Elijah.

I turn back around ignoring him as I walked towards the stairs. I passed by the kids rooms on my way to me and Gregg's room. I locked the door as soon as I stepped inside leaving my kids to fend for themselves. I had to get away from their curious stares, their now at the age where they can do for themselves.

"They will be fine" I said out loud to myself. Looking around our bedroom I noticed that the king size bed we shared was still unmade, the carpeting could use some vacuuming and there was no life in this room. Clothes were scattered everywhere, I walked right passed them and went to the radio and turned Pandora onto Vivian Green's station. I moved over to the windows overlooking our drive way and shut the blinds. I walked back over to my side of the bed, turned on the lamp and opened my night stand draw. Inside was a bunch of papers and the Bible. I moved everything to the side and lifted the bottom board and underneath was my blue marble crack pipe staring up at me. Next to it was a small clear package filled with crack pieces and an orange lighter. I took all the items took out and spread them on top of my night stand. I picked up the small package and began stuffing its contents into my crack pipe then lit it up. I kicked off my house shoes and swung my feet onto the bed and leaned back against the head board. I inhaled the smoke and allowed my body to relax. I didn't care if Gregg came home and smelled the crack. If he had a problem with what I was doing, then he could sleep his monkey ass on the couch. I wrapped my lips around the pipe again and tuned everything out as I reflected on the days of my childhood and how I met Thomas.

    Going back to my project life where I had a best friend Simone Blade, her family was well respected in Roger Williams Projects. Simone and I had been friends since we were three. Her father and my father were friends—our mothers well that was a different story, they disliked each other and they never told anyone why. At any functions we attended they kept their distance to keep the peace. Mrs. Blade treated me as if I was her own, despite her and my mother's differences, anytime I spent the night they bought me new pajamas and made sure I had three meals.

Mrs. Blade knew my parents were struggling to make ends meet and paying the rent on time was a constant issue. I recall a few times when Mr. Blade would come over saying he paid the rent for a few months. That's the only thing that didn't get around the projects. My mother didn't work and my dad worked for the housing projects we lived in doing maintenance work. Which didn't bring much to the table, so some nights my mother and I would dine on moldy bread for dinner and my dad would go to sleep hungry. Simone's family would bring food by to help us out and often I slept at the Blade residence.

The Blades never judged me or my family, it was never discussed how less fortunate we were. Simone had fancy clothes, shoes, jewelry, and the newest gadgets. I trusted Simone. She taught me how to be a lady. She told me I should always cross my legs, taught me how to do my make-up and my first kiss was because she taught me. We would stay up late when her parents went to bed practicing on each other. Simone was cool with everyone, so she got invited to all the good parties

I remember the first night we snuck out so vividly, because it was the first night I met Thomas personally. Simone had bought me a new outfit and made me change quickly. She did my hair in a high bun and did my make-up with a little mascara and lip gloss. We climbed out her second floor bedroom window and made our way down the fire escape, that Simone had pulled down earlier in the day. We climbed down until we couldn't anymore and one after another we jumped to the ground and took off running towards the direction of the party.

When we arrived at the party I was shocked, it was my first house party and as soon as the door opened we were welcomed by a cloud of smoke. Along with a crowd of boys and girls all zoned out and grooving to the music. I never smelled weed until that day. Simone got shown a lot of love as we moved further into the house, everyone was greeting her and I got the simple this is my *'friend Gail'* introduction. People gave me looks that said I wasn't supposed to be there and I was so uncomfortable, but I didn't want to let Simone down. She had a boyfriend named teddy, that she wanted to hook up with, so asked me to play wing man and I agreed. I sat in a living room while Simone took off with teddy and everyone else completely acted like I didn't exist.

There was a blunt in rotation and one of the guys next to me nudged my arm for me to take the blunt, I nodded it away. I sat there trying my best not to choke to death from all the smoke, when I noticed him walking into the party. He was light skin with eyes that look like honey and he rocked a Caesar cut. I could tell that he had a few years me over, but that's what made him even more attractive. He had on a white t-shirt and Roca wear jeans and I could tell by his time piece that he wasn't some regular nine to five working nigga. He looked down at me sitting on the couch as he passed by. I looked back up at him, it was the first time I felt butterflies and my palms started to sweat. He sat on the couch across from me and took the blunt out of rotation. He took a pull from the blunt and leaned back in his seat. The hairs on the back of my neck stood up because I knew he was watching me. I finally looked over at him again and became mesmerized by his eyes, they were sad and lonely with no emotion. He never once smiled just sat and stared. He held some type of respect because no one said anything when he entered the room, all eyes were to the floor. I was curious how anyone had that much control, it actually made me shutter a little bit. He looked at me like I was a trespasser. Everyone started getting up to leave, but none of them walked out without getting their approval from him first. Everyone dapped him up and left and we were left alone. I was holding my breath, I was uncomfortable and he just watched me. I crossed my legs and noticed they were shaking.

"Do I make you uncomfortable?" He askes.

I say nothing. I just look over at him. My heart was beating fast.

In sarcastic tone he says "I'm sorry do you not hear me speaking to you?"

I give off an attitude. "I don't know you boy, and I don't speak to anyone I don't know."

Next thing I knew he jumped up and smacked me across my face. I held my face in shock, my cheek stung like crazy causing tears to whelm up in my eyes. I couldn't even look at him.

He starts talking "You're sitting on my couch, in my house and calling me a boy? Have you not heard who I am? You ain't no different than these other bitches. You're going to respect me just like the rest of these motherfuckers up in here, you got that?"

Stuttering I say "Y-yes."

I'm crying at this point and he threw a dirty rag that was hanging on the arm of the couch at me, it landed in my lap.

"Dry them tears, I have no room for weak people around me."

The whole time I'm sitting there all I could think about was, could this really be happening to me? Simone never told me there would be guys who treat girls like this here. I felt so violated and ashamed, but I tried to suck it up because I didn't want to upset him anymore than he already was.

"Now let's try this again. What's your name?" He asked looking at me.

"Gail."

"Now where getting somewhere, I'm Thomas, but everyone calls me T."

I just sit there so confused like, how can anyone be so rude but handsome at the same time?

"So your Simone's friend?"

I nod and say yes and look him in the again. I could the knots forming all in my stomach as I try to keep it together. I was intimidated and turned on at the same time. I mean this guy just smacked the shit out of me and here I am sitting here feeling like I wanted to jump his bones. It was so weird and exciting at the same time.

"She didn't tell you I'm the guy here for you?"

I was confused and looked at him puzzled

"No!" I say. Curious to the news.

"Listen close, I'm only going to break this down once. You're going to be down with me. You're mine and I don't accept no as an answer, you understand?"

I'm confused still, sitting here like a deer caught in headlights. Simone basically set me up with someone who's apparently a drug dealer and a woman abuser. Now I'm his? This has become extremely frightening, yet I couldn't shake the excitement I was feeling from this man coming up in here and taking charge. He wasn't asking me anything, he was telling me. His hardcore demeanor had me wanting to know more about him. In my mind I already agree to his terms, but I don't say it out loud. Thomas intimidates me, yet his caress to my arm brought me out my thoughts and sent a chill down my spine. I never noticed him coming over to sit next to me.

"I need you to get focused. I need a loyal girl on my team and since your mine, I'm going to teach you the ins and outs. And once I see you can handle things on your own, I'll ease up with being around."

"What is it exactly that you want me to do?"

"Gail, I know you ain't stupid nor blind. I'm not going to sit here and sugar coat things for you. I push kilos of marijuana and crack and I have other females handling what I need handled. So what you're going to do is set up shop with me. You're going to cook up crack, learn how to weigh and distribute and make sure the money exchange is accurate."

I could feel him staring at me, but I don't look at him. Normal girls get first dates and flowers and stress over their first kiss, but not me. Questions are just flowing through my mind. My curiosity is at its peak and Thomas was the first guy to ever make me feel wanted and disgusted with myself at the same time.

"Also I need you to clean up," He looked at me from head to toe. "We are going to have sex and once you're comfortable doing that, you're going to seduce the men I tell you and as a reward I will give you the cut of the money and jewelry."

I gave him a blank stare. "Why me? There're plenty of girls out there. Why do you want to degrade me? My parents won't allow this. I won't allow this. I am only sixteen and I'M NOBODYS WHORE!!!" I scream out.

"First off you better watch your damn tone. Second I already told you what the deal is. I chose you and that's that, I don't give a fuck about your parents. I'll leave that up to you to handle. All I know is when I call for your services you better come running or that's your ass. Understood?"

I nod my answer as I picked up the dirty rag her threw at me earlier and wiped away the tears that had fallen from my eyes. He then reached inside one of his pockets and pulls out a knot of money. I've never seen that much money in my life. My eyes widen and I look over at him searching for answers.

"I'll take care of you Gail, just trust me." He then did the unthinkable and kissed me on the lips. Then hands me ten one hundred dollar bills. I took the money from his hand and stuffed it into my pocket and we both stand.

He says "I'll see you around." The plants another wet kiss on my lips. With multiple emotions running through my mind and body, I almost trip trying to get out of the door. When I left that night, I left Simone as well as our friendship behind.

I shake the thoughts of Thomas and how we met. I found it crazy how I had made him the man of my dreams, but in reality he was really my enemy. At least that's the way he acted. The way he talked to and treated me, was like he couldn't care less about me. But with the history that we have I made myself believe that it was just his way of showing his love for me. My crack pipe was no longer lit and I was out of crack. I needed more, I search for my phone. I needed to call my supplier.

Gregg

Speeding through traffic I cursed at the other drivers as I tried to get my brother to Rhode Island Hospital. Thomas was passed out in my back seat. I couldn't understand what caused him to pass out like that. We were having our usual drinks that we always ordered when we hit the bars, so I'm clueless to what is going on. I just didn't want to lose my brother. I pulled up to the front doors of the emergency room and put the car in park. I got out leaving the car running and ran inside to let one of the nurses know that I needed assistance right away. I'm sweating and my heart is beating so fast. Several nurses come from around the desk running.

I hear someone ask "What's the matter?"

Between breaths I say. "My brother! He's unconscious in my back seat. Please help him!"

I lead the nurses outside to my car where Thomas laid sprawled out in the backseat. One of the nurses were a male , so I asked him to help me get Richard out of the car and onto the stretcher that one of the female nurses and brought out. Once they had him strapped safely on the bed they rushed him back through the sliding doors of the ER and took him straight to the back. I wasn't allowed to follow suit, so I stayed put in the waiting room. A few minutes later a nurse approaches me asking me for Thomas' information.

I gave her as much as I knew and she asks me if I knew what happened. I tell her that we were out drinking and he just passed out.

"Ok well, just sit tight we will be back with you shortly." She said and walked back over to the front desk and began typing away at the keyboard of her computer.

I pulled out my cell phone to call my wife, but I decided against it. I really wasn't in the mood for her questions. So I decided to call Quan. Quan is Thomas's right hand man, he answered on the first ring.

"Hey brother man, something must be wrong if you're calling me." He chuckled.

I just ignored his sarcasm. "I need you to meet me at Rhode Island Hospital, Thomas passed out at the bar and I don't know what's going on."

"Say no more, I'll be there in five minutes. I'm right around the corner." He hung up on me.

Hospitals always made me sick and the air is so stale, there were pale green walls and off white tiles on the floor. There's a lot of chatter and chaos going on. I put my head in my hands and close my eyes and say a silent prayer.

"Lord, keep Thomas safe, I need my brother he's the only family I have, amen." I keep my eyes closed and try to keep my thoughts clear. The I felt a hand on my shoulder and I looked up, it was Quan.

"Any news yet bro?"

"Nah nothing yet." I sigh and stand up and we dap up. Quan took a seat in the chairs that were directly across from me. I sit back down

"How's that pretty little wife of yours?"

I shoot him a glance and see him with a half smirk on his face. "Is there a reason why asking?"

"Is there any reason why you just can't answer the question? I know it makes you uncomfortable."

Just as I was about to respond to that ignorant motherfucker one of the Doctors approach me.

"Mr. Greyston?"

"Yes?" I stand up and extend my hand to shake hands with him.

"Sorry I haven't had the chance to introduce myself, I'm Dr. Stanford. The attending physician, caring for your brother."

"How is he holding up?"

"He's stable and resting, we had to pump his stomach. He had a mixture of drugs and alcohol in his stomach contents which caused him to go unconscious. His vitals are stable. You should be able to see him shortly. I still have some concerns and questions. Maybe when he's alert and stable, we can ask those questions."

"Is there anything I could help you with?"

Dr. Stanford replies "I think we should just wait till your brother is stable, direct answers will be the best outlook."

"How soon can I see him?"

Dr. Stanford looked down at his watch then back at me. "I'll have one of the CNA's assist you to his room shortly, did you have any other questions for me?"

I told him I didn't and he extended his hand for me to shake it and told me that he would let the nurse know to escort me.

"Thank you doctor I appreciate everything." I watched as he walked off in the direction of where the nurses first rolled Thomas on the stretcher. I had no clue what was going on with the drugs that he spoke of, but I damn sure planned on getting to the bottom of it. There were a million thoughts running through my head right now, after taking in the news of my brother having drugs in his system.

I felt a vibration in my pocket. I look around the room and noticed that Quan was no longer here.

"I wonder where he went." I said out loud, then the vibration started again. I pull out the phone and realized that it wasn't mine. It was Thomas's phone, I remember placing it in my pockets when I was trying to get him out of the bar. Right as I was about to answer the phone stopped vibrating and a message popped up on the screen showing a missed call from 'G'. I shrugged and started to place the phone back into my pocket when it began vibrating again. The same name and number popped up, so I quickly answered before the person hung up again.

"Hello?"

"Uh…hello" The voice was very low and raspy, but it sounded quite familiar.

"Hello? Who's this?" I say again, then the line went dead. I could have been tripping because of everything that was going on, but that person's voice sounded awfully familiar. As I thought about it more and kept replaying the sound of the person's raspy voice in my head, I started to realize that it sounded like Gail's voice.

"Nah that can't be." I said to myself and immediately dismissed the thought. Moments later one of the nurses came to inform me that I would be able to see Thomas. I glanced around the ER to see if Quan had come back, when I saw that he was nowhere in sight still, I followed the nurse to Thomas's room.

Thomas

My eyes felt glued together when I tried to open them. I raised my brows in an attempt to stretch my lids and finally they opened. Looking around the room I noticed everything looked blurry, so I blinked a few times so I could see more clearly. My throat was aching, my mouth was dry, and I look at my arm and saw it had an IV in it. I looked up the bag is hanging from the pole and watched for a few seconds as the liquid dripped repeatedly.

How long have I been here? I thought. From the corner of my eye, on my left hand side, I saw something move. It was my right hand man Quan. He had his feet up on the medical supply cart and he was sleeping with a blanket thrown over him. Whatever happened to me must have been serious, because Quan would never step foot in any hospital. He always said that hospitals gave him the creeps. I tried to think back to how I got here and then I heard a *click*. The door to my room slowly opened and Gregg appeared from behind the small curtain that was drawn to block the door.

"Hey you're awake. How are you feeling?"

I cleared my throat and swallowed the bitter taste in my mouth. "I'm feeling ok, I guess. Just wish I had some water or something for my sry ass throat. How long have I been here?"

Gregg looked down at his watch. "A few hours. I brought you here late last night."

"What time is it now?"

"Seven a.m."

"Damn, What happened to me?" I asked trying to prop myself up in the bed. "The last thing I remember was taking shots with you."

"Yea and shortly after that you started complaining about being dizzy then you passed out. It was either that or you're getting too old and can't hold your liquor anymore." Gregg chuckled. I knew he was trying to make light of the situation. Ever since we were kids he would do stuff like crack jokes to help changed the bad aura in the room.

"Yea right nigga, I can still handle mines. I'll always out drink you, sick and all."

"I guess this situation hasn't done anything to your smart as mouth." Gregg smiled and shook his head.

"Ain't shit going to change, just my surroundings that's all." I replied. We went back and forth talking shit to one another for a while then the room grew silent. I noticed the change in Gregg's expression and body language and knew he had something on his mind. I figured whatever it was might've had something to do with Gail. I could tell he wanted to talk about it, so I took the bait.

"Wassup bro? What's on your mind?"

He rubbed the tip of his nose and licked his lips. "Uh, I was just thinking of something that doctor said to me before I came back here."

"What was that?"

"Well I had asked him how you were doing after they did what they had to do to you."

"Ok and?"

"And he told me that they had to pump your stomach for drugs." The lines in his forehead appeared. "Is there something you need to tell me?"

I rolled my eyes and looked at him with much agitation. "Gregg, if you there is something you want to ask me, then just ask."

He looked me right in my eyes and nodded. I watched him as he stood there looking like he was processing a million and one thoughts all at once. My chest began to rise and fall because I was becoming frustrated, not because he knew, but because I was in laying in a hospital bed when I could have been out making money.

Gregg stuck his hands in his pockets and looked over at me. "Are you doing drugs?" He finally asked.

He was expecting an answer and I was trying to think of one to shut him up, and make him move on from this topic. Just as I was about to speak one of the nurses walked in. I was saved from this awkward conversation.

"Hello Mr. Greyston. My name is Nurse Amy, I was coming in to check on you." She walked over to the right side of my bed and looked at the monitors. "How are you feeling?"

I turn my attention away from Gregg and tell her that I was feeling ok, just a little thirsty.

"Ok no problem I can get you some ice and water to help with that. Besides that are you doing ok?"

I shook my head. "Yes."

"Ok good. Well the doctor will be in shortly to speak to you and answer any questions you may have."

" Aight, Thanks."

"If you need anything else before then, just hit the button." She said pointing to the cord with a red button at the end. It was hanging over the side rails of my bed. She checked the IV bag and messed around with a few of the cords that were attached to me before leaving.

I looked over at Quan and saw that that nigga was still snoring. I was trying my best to avoid looking at Gregg, but he made it clear that he wasn't done. He started to say something when my room door opened up again and the doc walked in. Feeling relieved I exhaled and laid my head back again my pillow. Gregg turned to him and shook his hand, then he stepped aside.

"Hello Thomas, I'm Dr. Stanford."

"What's going on doc?"

"I am here to check your vitals. I know Nurse Amy was just in here, but it never hurts to double check right?" He said as he removed the stethoscope from around his neck.

"Right." I agreed and sat back up again.

He told me he just need to listen to my heartbeat and listen to my breathing.

"Take a deep breath for me."

I take a deep breath and he moves the cold metal to another area on my back. I sat there growing more and more impatient while the doc checked me out. All I could constantly think about was how much I wanted to get up out of here. When the doc was finally done he pulled out something that look like a pen, but then he twisted it and a light came on.

"I'm going to do an eye test, look straight ahead please." He said putting the light up to my eyes. I felt like a little kid getting an annual checkup or some shit. After he checked my mouth and did some other test he asked me how I was feeling.

"I feel fine, just ready to go."

He glanced over at the monitor. "Well, all your vitals look good and stable. You seem to be coming along pretty well. I just need to do some more tests on you and then we could see about getting you discharged."

"Ok cool, how soon will that be?"

"Well we did have to pump your stomach of substances and I am still waiting on a few of your lab work. I also want to monitor that small concussion you got from your fall too. So you can be out of here as soon as tomorrow morning."

"Tomorrow?"

Dr. Stanford nodded.

"Yo doc, check this out right. I don't have that kind of time. So why don't you just write me a prescription and let me be on my way."

"I'm afraid it's not that simple," Dr. Stanford began to explain. "With the substances we took from your stomach your digestive system could probably still be sensitive to any liquid or food intake, so before I can let you leave I have to be sure you will be able to keep your liquids and foods down."

He looked back and forth between me and Gregg, as if he had more news to share.

"What's up doc?" I asked.

"I just had a few concerns pertaining to the types of substances we found in your system."

"What kind of concerns?"

"The labs ran on those fluids showed that you had three different types of drugs in your system. Its policy that we offer the proper treatment and help to all patients battling any drug related addictions."

"Whoa, wait a minute doc." I had to stop him from saying too much. I already had Gregg burning a hole in my face with his eyes wanting to know if my dealings with drugs were true. I didn't need this damn doc coming up in here giving him more ammo on that. "I mean I may do recreational marijuana from time to time, but nothing else."

Dr. Stanford gave me a look like he wanted to question my response some more. I looked between the both of them. I saw Gregg unfold his arms like he didn't believe what I said, but that was my final answer and I was sticking to it.

"Thomas you had crack cocaine, marijuana, and traces of MDMH, also known as the street drug called molly in your system. This has the same contents of ecstasy. Now in order for me to help you, you must be truthfully honest and tell me how often you use these drugs."

"Man what?" I was becoming angry. I couldn't stand being accused of shit, whether it was true or not. What ever happened to patient/doctor confidentiality anyway? Last time I checked, Doctors weren't supposed to discuss certain matters in front of other people without the patient's consent.

"I have to ask."

"Well you don't need to ask me because I'm no addict and I don't do coke."

"Well is there a possibility that someone could have slipped something to you without your knowledge?"

I pretended to think for a while. I could still feel Gregg staring at me, I refused to make eye contact with him.

"I mean it could have happened, but I'm not sure when or by who. I move around a lot and I always around different people."

"Could it have been slipped into your drink at the bar by any chance?"

"I had two shots of Hennessey on the rocks I didn't notice anything unusual."

"Do you recall the bartender?" asked Dr. Stanford.

"I barely remember her." I shook my head trying to remember, but nothing was coming back to me.

"Could it be possible she put something in my drink?"

"Well she couldn't have because she would have put something in mine as well and I'm fine" Gregg butted in.

I looked at him and saw that the lines in his forehead were showing, I knew he was thinking.

"I remember her very vaguely didn't you get her number?" asked Gregg.

A light bulb clicked in my head. "That's right. Where are my clothes? Check in my jeans pockets."

Gregg crossed the room to where a clear bag filled with my clothes was sitting. He pulled out my jeans and something fell out my pocket. He looked down at the ground and bent over to pick it up. In a split second his expression changed to anger as he looked over at me and threw a small baggie filled with crack rocks at me.

I looked down at the baggie and back at him and asked. "No number?"

"Thomas explain the crack?" His voice was serious. His jaws were clenched. He was mad. In that moment he reminded me of our father. I had no intentions of letting him place me under his magnifying glass for examining, I'm my own man and I answer to no one. The doctor was still standing on my right side of my bed observing. Gregg was letting his emotions take control of him, and our personal issues were on display. I wasn't with all that.

"Doc can you give us a minute?"

He really didn't want to leave. He was waiting for an answer too, but at this moment it was best he take a walk.

"Sure no problem."

The moment Dr. Stanford exited the room Gregg charged at me snatching me up by my hospital gown. He twisted my shirt in his hands as he stared me in the face. Our noses were touching and his breathing was heavy.

"What the fuck is this Thomas?" He raises the clear bag, but I don't look at it.

In a calm tone I say. "Gregg you better take your hands off me. Just because I'm laid up in this bed don't mean I won't fuck you up."

"I'm in your face, so do what you gotta do." He snarled.

I reached up and snatched my shirt from his grip, then pull the IV out of my arm. I threw the covers back and shoved Gregg out of my face, he stumbled back trying to keep himself from falling down. By the time he got his footing I was out of the bed and rushing at him. I threw blow after blow to his body, trying my best to weaken him. We started scuffling and he managed to trap me in a bear hug shoving me back into a wall. I yelled for Gregg to get the fuck up off of me, but he wouldn't loosen his grip. So I bit him in the shoulder and grind my teeth until he finally let go. He backed away grabbing at his shoulder in pain. That's when Quan woke up and looked around to see what all the commotion was. He looked at me breathing all heavily and then over at Gregg who stood leaning against the wall nursing his shoulder and smiled.

"Looks to me the older brother is getting his ass handed to him by his younger brother." Quan started laughing.

Gregg glared over at Quan. "Shut the fuck up."

The whole time he was laughing I kept staring at Gregg. I was not about to take my eyes off of him and give him the opportunity to sneak me. With neither of us willing to back down we just stood there having a staring match.

"Gregg you're so pitiful bro." I spat.

"Take that dress off motherfucker and act like a brother and not like Thomas's father." said Quan.

Gregg ran over to Quan and picked him right up out of the chair by his throat. He slammed him up against the wall and dared him to repeat what he said. Quan tried to squirm free, but he couldn't break away from Gregg's grip.

"Who's wearing the dress now bitch?" Gregg says.

I ran over to Gregg and try to pull him off Quan. "Let him the fuck go Gregg, you want to fight someone? Fight me?"

I'm pulling his arms but he's not budging. The door to my room opens and we all look in that direction. I realize I'm still in a hospital gown and felt my ass was out, so I stepped back and cover my ass with the gown.

"What's going on Gentleman?" Dr. Stanford asked, shocked at what he was witnessing. "Mr. Gregg please let this gentleman down or I'll be forced to call the police."

Those words grabs Gregg's attention and he lets Quan go. Quan collapsed to the floor trying to catch his breath. Then Gregg walked over to me.

"Family Over Everything remember?" He throws my cellphone towards me and storms out of the room.

Quan

When Gregg called and said Thomas was in the hospital, my heart dropped. Thomas has been my best friend since we were kids. Thomas was the only kid at the play yard who never turned his back when I was picked on and bullied for being different. I didn't speak much, I played alone and my parents couldn't afford named brand clothing so I was disliked. Thomas took me under his wing, he brought me clothes and new shoes just so we didn't have to keep fighting every day. I always felt like I owed him for everything he ever did, but he would never let me repay him. Instead he said my loyalty was enough.

Thomas was the sibling that I never had, I grew up moving from house to house. My mother was a drug addict and my father started another family, leaving me behind. My grandmother took me in but was abusive and called me a bastard child. I constantly heard I was going to end up worthless like my mother. I would run away, steal food and sleep over at friends' houses that would allow me to stay. Some nights I even stayed in abandoned buildings. Christmas and birthdays were something I never looked forward to. My mom would take all the money and blow it on her addiction. She didn't care if there was food in the house, her life in the streets was more important. I learned to survive by stealing food, clothes and whatever else I could get my hands on. I got so good with stealing that I linked up with some boosters and started taking clientele. They would give me a list and I would steal what was on it. Stealing taught me a little bit of survival, but not enough.

  I was sixteen years old standing at 5'9 and weighing 155 pounds. I had dreads that hung to my shoulders, I was very skinny and had a smile to die for, at least that's what the ladies always say. I was fulfilling one of my clients list when I got bombarded by police. They had wanted pictures of me and my crew. They wanted me to rat out my friends, but I just copped a plea and took the five years they handed me. They handed me that much time because the amount of merchandise I stole met the federal crime. They sent me to the training school in Cranston, RI. Once I turned eighteen I was transferred to the Adult Correctional Facility where I served the remainder of my sentence. Thomas and I had lost touch, but we connected again. Some of the inmates were friends with him and let him know I was locked up that's how we got back in touch. A week later, I received a letter from him showing me love and letting me know he dropped a thousand dollars into my commissary. I didn't expect it but I was grateful. I got out of prison at the age twenty-one, that day when I walked out of the facility gates I was greeted by Thomas. He dapped me up and gave me a brotherly hug, then we rode off in search of some ass, because it had been awhile for a nigga. Ever since then we had been inseparable.

Forgetting about the streets, I made my way to Rhode Island Hospital. Weaving in and out of traffic, using no turn signals, I didn't care about nothing except making it to Thomas. My brother needed me and I was going to be there for him. I pulled up to the hospital and threw the valet my keys, as I rushed inside and marched right up to the receptionist desk. Some woman with a cheap weave and even cheaper ass lipstick was sitting at the desk. She looked like she could use a new weave and I could've whip that up for her real quick, but this wasn't the time for that shit.

"Can I help you?" She had the nerve to have an attitude and rolled her neck at me

I just shook my head and ignored her.

"Yea I'm here to see Thomas Greyston, he was admitted a little while ago."

"Sir, you can be seated in the waiting room and someone will be with you shortly" She said waving me off. I walk in the direction of the waiting room. When I turn the corner and I see

Gregg sitting with his head in his hands. The waves in his hair was so defined and his chocolate skin made me want to touch him. That was my dark secret that I kept buried and kept telling myself that this feeling would eventually pass. But every time I saw Gregg the butterflies and in my stomach would flutter, bringing out the femininity in me.

I was born Queenie Taylor on November 18, 1984. I knew inside I was always a boy, but after my Uncle molested me and my mom didn't care enough to protect me, things changed. I changed. I only wore boy clothes and I would tie my boobs down with ace bandages to make it look like I had no breast. I changed my voice when I spoke, so no one knew the difference. My hair was always nappy so I decided to dread it. When I got locked up, my lawyer fought for me to be sent to the boys Juvenile Detention Center and then be transferred to The Male Facility at the Adult Correctional Institution. They agreed and I was relieved, so I didn't have to explain the real me. Thomas I trusted him, but I still never let him know the real truth. Once he put me on to hustling, I paid for my surgery and took hormone pills. It took a couple years, but I'm fully a man now.

No matter how much I try to forget being born a girl, when I see Gregg it triggers my feminine side. It just made me want to touch him and caress his hair and kiss his soft looking lips. I did high school things just to piss him off so I could see the lines in his forehead come out. The way he clenched his jaws always turned me on, but Queenie was now Quan and I had to keep up with my façade. Gregg and I always argued like a married couple, he hated me. I don't know why, but he always threw shade my way and even then, I still wanted him badly. So bad that I was ready to give up this gangster life up and be the real me, be the woman I was born as.

Gregg never notice me walk away with the CNA, because he was talking to one of the doctors.

The CNA escorted me to Thomas's room without him. Upon entering room, I saw Thomas laying in the bed with his eyes closed. He had tubes in his nose and an IV in his arm. The sound of the beeping machines just brought a wave of sadness over me, and I fell to his bedside and start crying like a baby.

"Thomas if you hear me I need you, don't give up bro just stay strong." I sob a few seconds more and stop instantly. I take a napkin from the napkin dispenser and dab my eyes quickly. I didn't need anyone to walk in and see me crying like a girl. I pull up a chair next to the medical supply cabinet and sit down, because my feet were killing me. My toes were freshly manicured and painted the pink flamingo color that I loved. When I got it done everyone at the salon was staring at me like I was crazy, but I didn't pay them any attention. I made sure to go to a nail salon that was out of the area, had to make sure I didn't run into anyone who may know me. Anyway, I didn't want my toe nails to be smudged and I could feel it rubbing up against my sneakers. So to take the pressure off my feet I kicked them up on the railings of Thomas' bed. I sat there watching Thomas sleep peacefully, with his chest rising and falling slowly, until I found myself in a trance and eventually fell asleep myself.

It felt like I had only been asleep for a couple minutes, when I was awaken by the loudness of Thomas' voice. I thought I was tripping at first, but when I looked up and saw them tussling against a wall, I knew I wasn't. Thomas had bit Gregg in his shoulder and sent him cowering over in another corner of the room holding onto his shoulder. They weren't saying anything to each other, but from the looks of things, I assumed that Gregg must have found out about Thomas's drug use and wasn't very pleased. I never said anything about it, because that was Thomas's thing, even though he had offered me a few baggies of crack on several occasions. I never took him up on his offer. I was a good hustler I came from the streets, but one thing I didn't do was smoke my own product. If you do that then you're automatically destined for failure. I watched them have a stare off a little more, before I got tired of watching and decided to chime in. I deeply wanted to defend Gregg, but I owed my loyalty to Thomas. His side I took and it ended in me getting hymned up by Gregg. I had to admit I wasn't all that mad by it, in fact I loved every minute of Gregg choking me. I couldn't let that be known, so I pretended to fight back. The more adrenaline I used the more my penis rose. His muscles flexed beneath me and I was praying he dropped me before noticing the bulge in my jeans. The doctor came walking at the right time and ceased the commotion by threatening to call the police if Gregg didn't let me go. I smiled inside when the doctor came into and saved me from my embarrassment. Gregg dropped me to the floor and I start gasping for air. I made it more dramatic than it needed to be. The performance was worth an Oscar. Shortly after that Gregg threw something at Thomas after uttering a few angry words and stormed out.

"You good, bruh?" Thomas asks.

"Yeah, it wasn't nothing I couldn't handle." I told him rubbing my throat.

"Nah, Gregg be tripping, that shit ain't cool." Thomas punches the bed and I try to stand. The doctor lends me a hand and moved the chair closer for me to sit.

"I'm not tripping, but if he was any other motherfucker I would of been put him six feet under."

"Watch your mouth, motherfucker. I know he violated you, but you utter those words again and I will personally put you in the box. Right hand man or not, you got that?"

I knew he was serious by the tone of his voice. This is what disconnected me from Thomas a lot, because he treated me like a sucka' ass nigga.

I never fought him back because I had a hidden agenda.

"You right bro say no more, I'm just tripping." I tell him to make him chill out. Then my phone started to ring when I stood to extend my hand to dap my brother up and end the exchange of words. I look at the time saw that it was eight-thirty in the morning, who could be calling me at this time? My phone flashes *G.G. calling*. My eyes dart right over to Thomas. It was a form of betrayal I know, but him treating me like some punk bitch was equally betrayal.

I picked up and said. "Yea what's ups?"

"Hey baby can I see you?"

I was Gail's baby only when she needed something. Money or drugs was her usual, I couldn't blow my cover talking to Thomas's girl, so I continued talking like I was talking to one of our regs.

"What you need?"

Gail giggled she knew when I talked in code I was in the presence of one of her men. She didn't care she played along.

"I want you and that long black dick in my pussy." She giggled again and it sent chills down my spine. I took the phone from my ear because she was so damn cold. Those drugs took away the gentle woman I've gotten used to seeing preparing Sunday dinner in her Sunday's best while humming church music. Coming back to our phone conversation the woman on the other end was frail, tired and not looking her best.

"Yea I'll be there in 10 minutes."

"Where are we meeting?"

"The spot." I don't wait for a response I just hang up. "Ayo Thomas, I got to run man I have to go make this play real quick."

Thomas looks me over at me like he knew I was lying, but instead of saying what he really was thinking he just said.

"Aight, well stop by my spot and grab me some clothes and take these home." He hands me the clear hospital bag.

I take the bag and start heading to the door.

"Aren't you going to need the keys?"

I turn around, and he's tapping the key in his palm with his eyebrow raised. I couldn't look him in his eyes, I just grabbed the key and walked out the door. I pull my iPhone out of my pocket and go to my recent calls and call Gail. She answers on the first ring. I speak before she starts talking.

"No clothes just you and some heels." I hang up without listening to her response. Most people would judge me, but to hurt Thomas was a stepping stone for me to gain my respect and let him know I'm no little nigga and G.G. was a pussy with no face. End of story. I walked out the hospital to my car, started the engine and pull out into traffic.

Gail

    I found my car keys in the bottom of my purse and walked out into the hallway. I stopped in front of the mirror to check myself out. I hadn't looked this good in a long time, not that I had much reason to try to. I had my hair up in a high bun and I smelled like Victoria Secret's *Heavenly* from head to toe. I took my time shaving every part of my body that had hair. I pulled out my red lipstick from my pea coat pocket and smear it on my lips; I pull a tissue from the tissue box sitting on the little table under the mirror and folded it in half then kissed the tissue, I was ready to go. I tied the belt of my pea coat tight and looked down at my royal blue Zara heels, everything was intact. I head downstairs to the front door and walked out never saying goodbye to my kids.

    I got spooked earlier when Gregg answered Thomas's phone. Something must have happened.

I didn't care because I knew if Thomas didn't answer, Quan would. He would do anything to keep his tongue in my pussy and I didn't mind, because after all the sexing came my prize, crack. If it meant to betray everyone in my way, then so be it. Yes I loved Thomas. My heart has been with him since I was sixteen years old and when I moved, I cried myself to sleep every night praying that one day Thomas would find me. Finally the day came and my prayers were answered. Thomas walked back into my life.

The door to the Starbucks chimed but I didn't turn around, I was already running late for the bus to get to class. I was impatiently waiting to order my cappuccino when he came and stood beside me. I felt the hair on the back of my neck stand up. I didn't recognize him at first, but from the corner of my eye I seen that familiar smile I waited so long to see. My palms started to sweat and I couldn't believe it was really him.

"Do you mind if I buy you a coffee?"

I flashed a nervous smile, but I agreed. He pulled out a wad of cash from his pocket and paid for my coffee. I was embarrassed. I hated a flashy nigga, but Thomas was my world and him being here just confirmed he loved me too. My parents moved me out of the projects in my sophomore year in high school. My dad got offered a better job as janitor at another school, so he decided to move the family far away from the poverty stricken and violent life of the projects. My mom didn't say too much, she did whatever my dad asked. As for me, only being in high school at the time, I had no say so in the matter. I hated my parents. We moved to Boston, Massachusetts and I never expected to see Thomas again. Now here he was standing before me and looking finer than ever.

I never made it to class that day. Thomas and I ended up in the Holiday Inn in Brookline, MA. When I woke up it was dark. I forgot where I was until I turned over and seen Thomas. He was sleeping so peacefully. I didn't want to disturb him, but his legs were tangled between mine and I needed to pee. I moved his legs and he groaned.

"Where do you think you're going?"

I looked into his eyes and smiled. "Just to bathroom, baby."

"Don't be gone too long." He flashed a half smile "We were apart long enough."

I lean over and plant a kiss on his lips and sashay my naked body to the bathroom. When I came back out and walked back to the bed, something was sitting on my pillow. It was a small black box with gold trim. I was excited, but nervous at the same time. Could he be asking me to be his wife so soon? I turned my focus back onto the box and before I opened it, I looked over at Thomas. He has one hand behind his head and one hand on his belly watching the basketball highlights. He looked so handsome and so carefree. I opened the box and in it was a gold key, I looked at him and this time he was looking at me.

"Are you ready to leave mommy and daddy house?"

"When did you have time to make a key?"

He smirked a little. "You always have questioned my motives, I guess that smack when you was sixteen didn't set you straight."

He wasn't joking. He didn't smile. He had a straight face and looked me right in my eyes. I sat my naked body on the bed.

I responded slowly, "My parents won't allow me to move with you. They don't want me affiliated with any ties to those projects."

"Gail, I don't give a fuck about your parents. Do you want to be with me or not? It's not a complicated question."

"Yes Thomas, I want to be with you–but I can't turn away from school and my family their all I have."

"So what? Don't you have me? All this time you waited for me, now I'm here and you're having doubts?"

"How do you know I've been waiting for you?"

"We are on a need to know basis and this is one thing you don't need to know, so are you in or are you out?"

"I'm in Thomas, I love you."

He pulled my naked body to his naked tattooed body and spread my legs and kissed every inch of my body. We made love multiple times that I lost count. We never left the hotel that night and ended up ordering room service. Eventually we needed to come back to reality and get fresh air. I moved all my belongings out of my parents' house and my dad told me I was never to come back once he seen Thomas outside leaning on his rental. I was completely cut off from the Johnson family, but I had Thomas. Well at least I thought I did.

It was a Tuesday afternoon and we had just got finished having great sex. Lately I had been sleeping a lot more, but I think it was because I was drained from school and all the crazy sex we were having. I had 5 classes a day and I was in my second year, I didn't feel like attending class today so I stayed in bed. Thomas must have thought I was asleep because I could hear him in the living room talking.

"Yeah, I'm going to hook Gail up with Gregg it will work out perfectly. We will always have a source of income. Gail's job is to keep him occupied and monthly she is to make a deposit into my account. Gregg is running an accountant firm, his business was booming all the rich people trust him with their money. So since Gail is majoring in accounting she can get with Gregg and learn the business. Then eventually he'll let her handle the books alone."

I could hear him moving around and knew that he must have been pacing back and forth.

"...Bro, this is how it works. She wires a transfer of Five grand monthly, we come up with *twenty-five grand each month and re-up on our supply. Then split the cut fifty-fifty, we'll all eat."*

There's silence for a few minutes.

"Aight bro let me get this in motion. I'll be in touch"

Then he hung up. He didn't see me standing there, until he turned around and saw the look on my face.

"How much did you hear?"

"All of it Thomas." Shaking my head I say. "I can't believe you're willing to use me and your own brother to be on top. What kind of person are you?"

"I don't hear you asking questions when I'm putting stacks on the table for you to blow on shopping, or keeping your hair done and paying your tuition, where is your questions then?"

"I refuse to manipulate anyone especially your own flesh and blood."

Thomas jumped up and pushed me up against the wall, our nose touching.

"You are my bitch, you will do as I say. Fuck my brother, that nigga don't fuck me with anyways, he's always turned his nose up to me since we were kids. Now I'm going to do what I have to do to survive. You on the other hand will get your lazy ass dress and keep your head in those books. Find out what classes Gregg takes and get acquainted." From that day forward I was Gregg and Thomas's woman.

Now nine years later, I'm married with three kids to Gregg Greyston. We co-owned Greyston Accounting and our income is what most people would consider wealthy. We handled multiple million dollar accounts. We were well trusted, I handled the books just like Thomas requested and I wired the money faithfully. I was angry because Thomas had said this was temporary. It was damn near a decade and I'm still not back home with him. There are other women sleeping in my bed and when I confront him, he always tells me my place is with Gregg and I need to keep focus on that. Little by little, he was giving me crack. At first I declined, but his new thing before sex was to smoke crack. He would tell me how amazing our sex would be when he did it, so I decided to try it and he was right. Six months later, I became addicted and that was Thomas's new way to shut me up. I enjoyed my lifestyle with Gregg but I preferred to spend my days with Thomas. This new control tactic made me smoke more and not care about my place anymore. I was losing my patience and my love was turning into an addiction for Thomas and the crack. I was completely destroying a man because of the jealousy and greed of his own brother.

  I get out of my thoughts as I pull up to the spot, me and Thomas's shared condo. I pull out my key from my glove compartment and let myself in. Right at the front door was clear baggies neatly placed in a trail. I picked up each baggie, as my mouth watered. I followed the trail to the end of the hallway where Quan sat with his dreads pulled back and the candles flickering. I could see he was wearing a wife beater, twirling the last baggie in his hands. I stop in front of him.

"Take that coat off" Quan demanded.

I untie my pea coat and let it hit the floor. Quan is sizing me up. I was still petite, my nice breast size stayed in place and my ass still caused necks to break, because I had a small frame. Quan and I made eye contact as I seductively licked my lips and blew him a kiss. He stood up and grabbed me by the neck and stuck his tongue down my throat. We catch a breath in between and I drop to my knees and take his penis in my mouth. I'm looking up at him, he's watching me as I slide his penis deeper and deeper into my throat. The sloppier I made his penis the more I became moist between my legs. I create more saliva and work his penis in and out of my mouth as I massage my clit vigorously. Quan put his hands on the back of my head and started humping my face faster and faster. I knew he was about to cum, so I pulled away and stood up. His chest was heaving and he was ready to blow, but I wanted him to wait. I turned around and held on to my ankles and waited for him to slide inside of me. He followed my lead and spread my ass checks apart, so he could see my vagina wrap around his penis. I knew how to tighten my muscles and contract them just the way he liked it, so I worked my magic and rode Quan with every pump he gave me.

"I'm about to come, Baby." Quan said pumping harder.

"No baby not yet" I pull away again and he's frustrated I get back down on my knees and let and finish him off like that. He's pumping harder and my face is getting sore, but I don't stop. He holds my face by my ears becoming more aggressive, but I still continue to work him. Then he puts his hand on my throat and I continue to pleasure him even though I couldn't really move. Quan was gripping my throat too hard and I was starting to feel dizzy. He continues pumping and I start digging my nails into the sides of his buttocks, but he just goes harder. Then finally, he pulls his penis out and cums all over my face. I felt so disgusted, dizzy and weak. Quan pushed me out of his way as he walks off and begins adjusting himself. I sat there on my knees with my eyes closed and held my throat trying to catch my breath. I realized then that I hadn't eaten in damn near two days. I felt humiliated still sitting here with nut on my face, but at this point my main goal was to get high and erase what Quan just did to me, out of my mind. I catch my breath and grab up my pea coat and the baggies of crack, then head down the hallway to the bathroom and lock myself inside. I turned on both the hot and cold water to wash my face. I grab for the towel and dry my face, then dug into my coat pocket to find my lighter and crack pipe. I stuffed my pipe with crack and lit it up and smoked my problems away.

Gregg

    I finally made my way home after the fight with Thomas and that bitch ass nigga Quan. I had to get out of their before I ended up in a situation I couldn't come back from. I drove around Providence to calm my nerves, I didn't want my kids seeing me like this but I had to go home. I needed rest and a shower. As I'm coming up my street I see Gail in a pea coat climbing into her car. I slow down and pull over to my left so she wouldn't see me. She reversed out of her parking spot and passed by me. I quickly put my car in drive and busted a U-turn and followed her. She weaved in and out of traffic. She never was a good driver, but I was able to stay two cars behind her. Once we hit the exit I knew exactly where we were heading. We took the Hartford avenue exit. We were headed to Thomas's house. Questions were overtaking my mind. How long had Thomas been sleeping with my wife? When did they have time to talk? Shit wasn't adding up. My biggest fear was looking me dead in my face. My wife was betraying me, except it wasn't with Thomas because he was laid up in the hospital. So, who drove the grey charger? I caught a glimpse of the license plate when I was able to get close enough and saw that it definitely looked familiar. I watched Gail get out the car, walk up to the door and let herself in. When did she get a key? It took everything in me not to go inside and kill her, but it was 10 a.m. and I needed to get home to my kids. They had been home alone and I knew they were probably wondering where the hell their parents were. Every question that was raised in my brain made me angry and my tension was building. I stepped out of my car and crept around to the side of the house and peeked through the window. I could see Gail picking something up off the floor but I wasn't able to tell what it was. I saw some dim lights flickering off the wall and that's all I needed to see, it didn't take a genius to know what was about to happen next. Shaking my head in frustration I went back to my car and headed home. The drive to my house was completely silent, no music, no phone calls. Just me and my million and one thoughts.

    I pulled into my driveway feeling angry and betrayed. I knew my kids were going to be up, especially waking up to both parents not being home and most likely they would be asking where their mother was. I put my key in the lock, turn the knob, and walk in. It was quiet. I walked through the living room towards the kitchen, greeting me at the kitchen table was Isaiah. He had that look of worry in his eyes, it made him look like his mother. He resembled her a lot with his light skin, medium build and head of neatly twisted dreads that hung past his shoulders. He was always mistaken as an older kid. He was tall for his age, very mature and humble. He didn't speak on much unless it was really necessary. I admired that about him.

"Wassup pop is everything okay?"

"Yeah, why do you ask son?" I knew the answer. He's an observer so I knew where this conversation was heading.

"Dad you've been gone all night, and mom didn't eat she just stayed in the bedroom. I could smell a funny odor coming from your room and then she left at 9:45 this morning, is something is going on?"

"Son I have never lied to you, so I'm not going to start. You're of age to understand marriages have issues, you understand right?"

Isaiah said nothing he was just staring at me waiting for me to continue.

"Well son, I don't know what's going on with your mom. I believe she's having an affair and the books at the firm are missing money. Something's going on and I'm going to get to the bottom of it. Just give me time, son"

"Dad, I goggled foaming at the mouth, it's a side effect from not getting their fix on drugs, is mom on drugs?"

I was shocked by his question, because I had no idea that my kids were able to see the things I've been noticing about their mom.

"Your guess is as good as mine, Isaiah. You don't need to worry, son, as the man of the household it's my job to take care of this family and fix this and keep us together." I looked over at Isaiah to see if I assured him, but his eyes were on me. For a moment I saw my dad staring back at me, like when I first brought Gail home. He sensed her disloyalty then.

Isaiah had more questions, but I didn't let him get them out. I was exhausted and I needed a shower. I stood up and walk over to where Isaiah is sitting and put my hand on his shoulder. He doesn't look up at me. He's just staring at my empty chair.

"Isaiah, I will handle it. In the meantime, you have a younger brother and a sister upstairs who needs you and I need you. Keep your head together, we will get through this."

His eyes finally met mine and I knew he heard me. I walked to the stairs and took them two at time, I needed to be alone with my thoughts. I opened the door to our room and the smell and fog lingering in the room smacked me in the face. I knew the smell of pot and this defiantly wasn't that. I shook my head in disgust and walked over to the window to open it so some of this nasty smell could get out.

Just yesterday, I had a family and now here I am watching it slip through my fingers. I sit down on Gail's side of the bed and lay back. I was drained and I just wanted to erase the events of this day. I put my hands behind my head and I felt something rubbing against my skin, so I grabbed it. To my surprise it was a small clear plastic bag with tiny white particles in it. My thoughts were confirmed. My wife was a functioning crack head. I was highly disgusted, this was the exact reason why my mother is not a part of me and Thomas's life. Gail knew this. Our life, her life is a façade.

I opened the drawer to her nightstand and began rummaging through it. I wasn't sure of what I was searching for exactly, but I figured an answer to why she was destroying our family would be in there somewhere. The drawer smelled just as strongly as our room did when I first walked in, I just snatched the draw off its track and threw it against the wall. The drawer broke into pieces and out fell ashes from an ash tray and a yellow envelope. I picked up the envelope noticing that it was addressed to no one, so I tore it open and inside was two sheets of paper from the DNA Diagnostic Center, my heart dropped as I began to read it.

Dear Mrs. Greyston,

We have received your DNA report and are writing to inform you that the results of your paternity test are as follows:

Isaiah Greyston 99.9%

Elijah Greyston 00.0%

Naomi Greyston 99.9%

Vs.

Thomas Greyston

I couldn't read anymore, a tear rolled down my face. I held the letter and fell to my knees and cried like a baby. I was a broken man. My kids belonged to my brother and I was living every man's nightmare of betrayal. I cried and punched my fist into the floor pleading to God to explain why. I didn't know how long I was on my knees, I just knew that I wanted answers and either Thomas or Gail was going to give it to me. I was raising children that weren't mine. I was their uncle.

    I had to seek revenge, I been the joke of this family to long and now it was my turn. I was going to have the last laugh. I got up from the floor and headed down stairs to the kitchen where I retrieved a trash bag from beneath the sink. I wanted every piece of Gail out of my sight. I hated her and I refused to let her live in my presence another day. I would handle Thomas next and if Quan gets in my way, I will kill him with my bear hands. I realized she was driving the car that was in my name and has access to the firm and to our bank accounts. I pulled out my cellphone and Goggled the number to the locksmiths. Once I found one that didn't require an appointment, I let them know I needed emergency service immediately. I made a request for them to change the locks to my home and firm right away. I even offered to throw in an extra fifty dollars if they could do it within the next hour. That way I would be left with enough time to get to Citizens Bank. I got right in and out of the bank since I was the primary account holder, I removed her name without any issues. I wanted so badly to call

Thomas, but I was on my own. I hurried back home to meet the locksmith.

An hour and a half later all the locks were changed, and I had a mission to complete that required a little help from Isaiah, although I preferred for him not to be involved. I found Gail's spare key to her car and called Isaiah downstairs.

"Wassup pops?"

Hearing him calling me pops sent a blow to my stomach, but I kept my composure.

"I hate to have to involve you but I need your help with something."

"What's that?"

"I need you to drive your mother's car home."

"Why? What's wrong with it?"

"Nothing, listen I'll explain everything later. Could you just do me this favor?"

Isaiah shrugged. "Sure, whatever you need pops,"

"Ok good now go put your shoes on and let's take this ride."

He walked away and another tear slid down my cheek. I wiped my tears away this wasn't the time for me to show any signs of weakness.

We jump inside my car, buckled up and headed toward the highway off Cedar Street in Pawtucket.

"Are we going to Uncle Thomas' house?"

I looked at him, how did he know? He was smarter than I thought. I ignored his question and kept my focus on the road pondering if I should tell him about the paternity results.

"Are you going to tell me what's going on pops?"

"Are you ready to hear the truth son?"

"Pops, I'm a grown man, don't child proof the truth, I'm all ears."

I look at him and he was burning a hole in me for an answer, I let out a sigh and began.

"Your mom is a functioning drug addict and she is having an affair with your fa-...I mean you uncle Thomas" I caught myself before saying it out loud. I looked over at him. He was watching the road, his face was emotionless and I figured he was soaking everything in, so we rode the rest of the way in silence.

We arrive at Thomas's house in Washington Park. I turn the engine off then turned to face Isaiah.

"Son, do you have any Questions for me?"

"Yeah, why are we sitting here?"

I'm a little taken back by his cold tone, but I let it go. "I need you to take this key," I held up the Nissan spare key and he tries to take it from my hands, but I pull back. " I want you to take this key and take your mother's car home. Understood?"

"Yeah, pops, I understand." He took the key from my hand, opened the door and got out.

"Hey!" I say and he turns around. "I love you, Son."

He nods and shuts the door. I watched him walk across the street to Gail's car, unlock it and hoped in starting up the engine. I cut my engine back on and signal him to pull out in front of me, he does so and we head home.

Thomas

"F.O.E." I said aloud after I was finally left alone. I'm sitting here reflecting on Gregg's words to me as he stormed out. "Where was this so called family when I was raped by the neighborhood babysitter's husband?"

The anger rose in my chest as I took a seat in the chair in the corner of the room and rubbed my chin. Thinking back to the day it all started.

When I was nine years old. He, who's name I don't care to mention, use to flash me when no one was around or looking. I would always ignore him and pretend that I didn't see anything. Staying by his wife's side was my only guarantee of safety ,she was like a mom to me and he would always call me a sissy and say I needed to put on a dress. I was a child looking for the love and comfort my own mother never gave to me. The first time it became physical, I had to stay with them while my dad went out of town. Gregg handled my dad's business and had no time to babysit his kid brother. So I was stuck with him where I spent many nights crying myself to sleep after he had crept into my bed. I recalled one night when I was asleep in my room. I was wearing a pair Captain America underwear and no shirt. I was awakened by him stroking my back and staring down at me with a nasty smile on his face. I was so nervous and scared of what he might do to me if I tried to scream, so I didn't utter a word. He picked me up and laid me on top of his lap and continued stroking my back. I was shaking uncontrollably with fear, but he just kept on touching me. He made me sit upright in his lap and when I did he began grinding against me. I began to cry as he placed me back in my bed and start to unbuckle his pants. My mind was telling me to scream for help, but I couldn't force any sound from my lips. He seemed to be turned on by my crying because he dropped his pants and began stroking his manhood and making weird noises. Then he reached down and stuck his hand in my underwear and started touching me too. Him touching me made me feel sick to my stomach and I pissed all over his hand. He pulled his hand back and grimaced at me, I knew he was mad and I was afraid because I thought for sure that he would beat me. But he didn't, instead he made me get up and pull the sheets off my bed. Once I did that he made me bend over and everything after that was a blur, all I know is that the next morning when I woke up there was a fifty dollar bill under my pillow. I must have been so scared I passed out, whatever the case was that night, I took that fifty dollars and stashed it in my backpack. Then I got dressed and left. I purposely to stayed away from the house during the day and returned back in time to speak to my father, who would call to check in on me. One day when I came back to the house and he was sitting in the living room. I became scared and looked around for Mrs. Ang, but she was nowhere to be found.

"Where you been boy?" He asked.

"Nowhere." I mumbled and started to head for the stairs, but he had gotten up so quickly and had me cornered near the front door. He reached down and grabbed ahold of my penis and began massaging it through my pants. I tried to move his hand away, but he held on tighter and the more I squirmed the tighter his grip became. I peed on myself again and he finally let go. I stood there scared with urine trickling down my legs and into my shoes and socks. We here a sound somewhere else in the house and he looked in that direction. The he turned to walk away from me, as soon as he did I run passed towards the bathroom.

"Thomas, are you okay?"

The sound of her voice made me feel safe, I unlock the door for and see Ms. Ang standing there with a worrisome look on her face. She entered the bathroom and reached out to me.

"Are you ok baby?" She asked again after noticing how badly I was shivering. "What happened to you?"

I wanted to tell her so bad, but I couldn't bring myself to do so. She noticed my wet clothes

"Is this why your hiding? You had a little accident, nothing to be ashamed about." She rubbed my arm "Take a shower and I'll get your pajamas and then you can have some apple pie and ice-cream before bed."

I nodded and hopped in the. I washed quickly because I wanted that pie, because Mrs. Ang's cooking was the best. I dried off and put my pajamas on and walk out in the kitchen to find Mrs. Ang and him having sex right there in the kitchen. He realized I was watching and flashed me a grin. I no longer had an appetite. I went straight to bed, only to be woken up to him in bed with me again.

"Did you like what you seen today?" He whispered. His breath smelled like shit and liquor

I wanted to puke. His hands were caressing my legs and I'm shaking hoping he would stop, but he never did. He pulled my pajama pants off. I lay there on my back cupping my penis, crying and praying that someone saves me. He began taking his clothes off. I'm too nervous to run, I'm scared and he seems to enjoy my fear. The rest was a blur, but when I woke up I was in a pool full of urine and feces. My butt hurt when I sat up.

I still never told anyone until I was older. When I confided in Mr. Blade, Simone's dad .I tried numerous times to tell my own father, but he told me I was a kid and I was making up stories. I never allowed anyone to hug me again it always made me flinch.

One day my dad asked "Are you afraid of me?"

I never responded because I was angry with him. I felt like he didn't protect me like he should have and I despised him.

Mr. Blade, on the other hand took action. I was fifteen and we were sitting in Mr. Blades Business office and he let me have my first drink. After a few I just confessed. He never said anything, just listened. When I was finished he put his drink down on his cherry wood desk, walked over to his safe and took out what he called a "duce duce." It was a little chrome .22 revolver. I never held a gun before, but he told me I needed protection and I knew what he wanted me to do.

I prepared hard for this day. I didn't involve anyone I wanted to handle this on my own. It was the beginning of October and nights were getting colder, so me having on a black hoodie didn't draw any attention. I waited till night fell and crept up to Mrs. Ang's house and right on schedule, he was sitting in his chair with his glasses on reading the Providence Journal. I walked right into their house, the door was never locked and pointed the .22 at him. He looked at the barrel of the gun without any hesitation. He folded his paper neatly, took off his glasses and placed them on the end table. He took a sip out of the glass and sat back and looked me right in my face. I'm frozen but I wasn't turning back, this man stole my youth and violated me.

"I knew I would pay for what I did to you eventually, I love you son"

I let off two shots straight to his head. He was no father to me. I took off out the front door, fading into the night. A year later I found out he really was my father, Thomas Jenkins. He had money saved for me and a lawyer came by one day to have me and the man who I thought was my father sign the paper work for the money. I was in shock, I had killed my own father.

I come out of my thoughts and took a sip of the water that was sitting on my bedside table. I sat back wondering what was taking Quan so long. I wanted to call Gregg, but our fight had me saying fuck him. We never really had a relationship until after he returned from college with Gail on his arm. Gail and I acted so nonchalant like we had never met. I trained her well enough and she played her role very well. Unfortunately, my step dad sensed her disloyalty and turned his nose to her. Meeting Gail at that party when we were kids was a setup to keep her close for Mr. Blade. I never intended on hurting Gregg, but we never had a brotherly relationship until recently. When the payments Gail were supposed to be making went into a default I needed to keep Gregg close.

Gregg was always considered the good brother. Everyone loved him. Me, I was what you would consider the bad apple of the family. I spoke with foul language, I wore my pants half off my ass, and I held no hesitation with smacking anybody around who I felt was being disrespectful towards me. Gail and I had a long history. I kept my eyes on her since she was a little girl. Coming over to Blade house in her dingy clothes and matted hair. Mr. Blade had informed me that

Gail's father had an unpaid debt, and if he didn't pay she was to pay and he was going to handle Malcolm himself. Everything played in my favor once I came back into her life and they immediately cut all ties with her. Mr. Blade was given six months to live after fighting cancer for several years and he decided against chemotherapy, but his time lately was coming sooner than later. The last time I seen him before he passed away, he requested I come to the hospital alone because he didn't trust Quan. He said that from day one.

I show up at the hospital, and he hands me a paper with Gail's address. I knew it very well since I found out where she had moved to on my own. He pulled me in for a hug and whispers to me.

"Handle this for me."

I look him in eyes and said nothing, I knew he meant business and I would never go against the grain, not when it came to loyalty. An hour after I left I got the call that he had passed on. He was just hanging on for me. I cried like a baby. Mr. Blade was my Father, the man who taught me to be a man and out of respect, I was added as his son in his eulogy. The Blades were my family and I would never let anyone say different. Mr. Blade had been preparing me to be the next man in line of calling the shots from Prairie Ave to Comstock, but I had one duty to fulfill and that was to take Malcolm Jenkins out. Thomas Jenkins and Malcolm Jenkins were brothers, which made me and Gail cousins. It was already too late to turn back now, they were no family to me at all. Malcolm always disliked me, and I never gave a fuck. Whenever I ran into him he would walk in the other direction and I would laugh. He only hated me, because my mother betrayed his brother and let another man raise me as his own. It all made sense why Malcolm did not want me around Gail, because I knew of the family secret, I was one of them. Once Gail fell in love with me Malcolm no longer had control and his anger and bitterness got the best of him and he turned his back on his only kid.

Gail was a pawn in my chess game, so I needed her and once I took her back to the south side I had her right where I wanted her. I had planned my attack on Malcolm. I had approached Malcolm on different occasions about his unpaid debt to Mr. Blade before bumping into Gail at the coffee shop. He laughed me off and told me to stay away from his family. I would walk away leaving him with silence. I was never one to send an empty threat, I had the address in hand and I called up Quan.

"Yo, I need you to make this move with me real with quick."

"Wassup bro, you good?"

"Not over the phone, meet me on Comstock in five"

"Alright bet." He replies. We hang up.

I turned on Comstock and pull up next to his Gray charger. I roll my window down.

THE FACADE

"Get in." He looks at me crazy, but never asked a question. Quan jumps in and I take off towards Boston, never once did Quan ask where we're going. We pull up at Malcolm's House, park and I pull out an untraceable tracfone. I called the number to their house phone and Malcolm answers on first ring.

"Do you have my money?"

"How did you get this number?" I could tell he was nervous.

"One more time, do you have my money?"

"I told you to stay away from my family you—"

I hung up, his time was up. Quan and I step out of the car. I pop the trunk pull out two gasoline cans and hand one to Quan, then walk right up to the house. We poured gasoline on and all around the house. We lit matches, tossed them and watched the fire rise and light up the dark skies. We ran back to the car and I peel off back to Providence. I was heading home to Gail.

I climb right behind her into the bed and slide my penis into her moist vagina. She moaned and I go crazy, not feeling not one ounce of remorse for what I had just done. Malcolm's debt was now Gail's and marrying Gregg was the best way to keep her close and always having access to money. She had no idea what was going on, she thought this was to build for me and her, but I didn't love Gail. Because I felt that she would betray anyone and if she could betray Gregg, she could betray me too. I was no fool.

"Thomas, are you alright?" I look up to see Quan standing in front of me. I didn't know how long I was in my thoughts. I see my blue Nike duffle bag hanging over his shoulder. Something wasn't right, I felt it.

"Where you been nigga?"

"I was checking out the block. I had to make sure everything was moving smoothly." He hands me a stack of cash. From the looks of it was about six grand, four grand short.

"Where's the rest?"

He looked at me confused. "It's all there, you can count it."

"How much is supposed to be here Quan?" I knew it wasn't right to question him, but my money was short and I needed an answer.

"Its six grand, Thomas."

"Wrong! When I check in and collect money its ten grand, so where the fuck is my money?" He had no answer. "I'm going to give you an hour to get my money or I'm putting two holes right in your head."

He doesn't argue with me back.

"I need to get to my car it's still at South Street."

He finally speaks "Get dressed bro, and I'll drop you to your car."

Gail

I smoked and fell asleep on a cold tiled floor. I look around, coming to my senses of where I was. I was in me and Thomas's half bathroom. I looked for my phone, checked the time it read 3 p.m. I vaguely recalled what happened last night, but all the money laid around me brought some clarity. I had taken the money from Quan's pocket after he violated my face. What a better way to make him pay. I try to stand up and I stumble a little to the side. I'm still a little bit groggy, but I need to smoke. I open my bag in search for my pipe. I flip my bag upside down and everything inside falls to the floor. I see it lying by the trash can. I reach over and grab it and look for another bag of crack to stuff the pipe and light up. When I found it I felt relieved and smiled when I saw the white clouds of smoke form from me lighting the rocks. I inhaled deeply and enjoyed the feeling that consumed me when the smoke entered my lungs. I keep repeating the process until there was no more. All the clear baggies were in front of me, empty. I was so upset and losing control fast. So, I opened up the cabinet under the sink and found a can of Ajax bathroom cleaner. I'm desperate and it's close enough to crack. I stuff my pipe and light it up. I pull back and inhale, it sends me into a coughing attack. I catch my breath after almost coughing up a lung and try to stand again using the sink for balance. I saw my face in the mirror and I realized that I was naked. I took a cup from the dispenser and drink some cold water hoping that it would help ease the tightness in my chest. I didn't look like the woman from last night. My eyes were blood shot, my hair was all over my head and my lips were dry and cracked. I didn't care about my looks at this point. I scooped up all the contents from my purse and the money from the floor and put it back in my bag. I grabbed my coat and heels open the bathroom door and lay them on the table.

I go into the bedroom and find an old t-shirt on the top shelf in the closet. When I pulled the shirt out a black book and newspaper articles fell out too. I knelt down and scooped up all the newspaper articles and one caught my eye. The heading read: ***Couple Killed in a House Fire.*** I pulled the article out of the bunch and opened it up. My parent's picture was staring back at me, all sorts of emotions were running through me all at once. Nausea was the strongest one, I ran over to the trash that sat near our dresser and threw up. My parents were dead and I didn't even know about it. I kept my head in the trash until my vomiting turned into dry heaving. How long had Thomas Known? Did he have something to do with this? When was the funeral? Still completely naked I walk back over to the newspaper articles and put on the t-shirt. I sat down Indian style and slowly picked up the clippings and read them again. Tears came streaming down my face once I read the date *October 17, 1996*, its 2013. I just cried and cried, because I never got to say goodbye to my parents. The pain in my heart was unbearable and I was in a ball of sadness. I needed Thomas to explain why he never told me my parents passed away. Why did he have these clippings stashed away? I got up and took the clippings with me. I head out of the bedroom and back to where my belongings were and put on my coat. I grabbed my bag and put on my heels, find my keys and head out to my car.

I walk out front and my car is no longer there. I look up the street to the right and down the street to the left my car is nowhere in sight.

"What the Fuck!" I stomp my foot. I can't call Gregg he'll want to know why I'm over here at a Thomas's house. I don't feel the need to explain myself these days, so I take off heading towards Eddy St. trying get to Taylor St. That walk in heels felt like forever, so along the way I stopped and took my heels off. I didn't care I was on a mission I had four grand in my purse , my parents were dead and I had no crack today. I didn't give a fuck about life. I knew where I could get crack from, there was always some of Thomas's workers who sold 24-hours out the day. So I made my over to Taylor St. and some of the young dudes I've seen come to the house were out there.

"What up Mrs. G? Thomas know you out here?" One of the young boys spoke.

"Fuck Thomas, which one of y'all is holding?" I see a bunch of confused faces. "Which one of y'all is holding the crack?" I see the hesitation.

"No disrespect Mrs. G, but your Thomas' girl and he's our boss, we can't sell to you he'd kill us."

"Like he killed my parents" I mumble. I pull out the four grand that was all crumbled up, all eyes were at attention, money always had a way of changing things. One young boy stands up.

"Man fuck Thomas! Money's money, it still spends the same no matter where it comes from, crack head girlfriends and all."

A few of the fellas looked at him like he was crazy and a few nodded and agreed. I had to pee in that very instinct and didn't see anywhere I could go really quick, so I pulled my coat up and hung my bag on the fence, and squat down to piss.

"Man Mrs. G this ain't right. What you doing?"

"What it look like motherfucker? What you ain't ever seen grown woman pussy before?" I stand up and shake the last bit of pee and laugh in his face, he backs up with a face full of disgust.

"How many of you young boys want to tap this old pussy?" I do a little spin showing off my vagina with no panties.

"Pussy is pussy come up here with us" said one of the fellas. I snatch my bag off the fence and it rips. I storm up the steps they were sitting on and they lead the way inside. There were two more guys inside sitting on the couch counting money and separating drugs.

"Yo, what the fuck are you doing with T's Girl?" One of the guys says.

"She's down to fuck."

The guy steps back and throws his hands up like he didn't want any parts. "If T come after you, I can't save you. You're going to take this fall without the team."

The guy who lead me in the house shot back "Man I'm tired of you niggas. What you scared of that nigga T? If he was in this situation he would be doing the same thing, so fuck him! I'll deal with him when he comes for me, till then I'm going to fuck his bitch." He grabs me by my hand and leads me to the basement it was cold and drafty. The boy said "Take off that shirt" I stripped as he said. "Get on your knees hoe."

I followed every command. His penis entered my mouth and I felt someone enter me from behind. I didn't stop them from running a train on me, I just maintained my stamina because I knew once they were done with me I would get my crack and be on my way. It never crossed my mind that they had other plans for me.

I was zoned out and by the time I realized they were finished with me, I was outside banging on the door crying. I was naked. They had robbed me and took the four grand I had taken from Quan. They left my bag next to me, but my cellphone was missing and I couldn't call anyone for help. Nobody was outside like earlier and I just sat on the stoop thinking while people passed staring at me. I'm sure I looked crazy, but I didn't care I just needed my high. I lay my head in my lap, and doze off into a sleep. I'm awakened by a shake to my shoulders.

"Ma'am are you ok?"

I moan and roll my head to the right and it's a cop.

"Ma'am? What are you doing out here? Where are your clothes?"

I was confused on where I was, and I was feeling sick. I realized I hadn't eaten in damn near two days.

"Do you have a name, mam?" I look at the bald black cop "Do you hear me? I need you to come with me this is indecent exposure, and I have to take you down to the precinct."

I finally speak "Is it really necessary to take me to jail?" I try to stand up, but apparently I'm still high and miss a step. I fell down six steps scraping up my knees and my hands are bleeding. My face hit the pavement and I had an open gash on my eyebrow. The cop tried to catch me, but it didn't help. The cop goes to his trunk and gets me a blanket and helps me stand. He walks me over to the backseat where I see a crowd of people watching. I just bow my head and duck into the backseat. He hands me a few gauze, to help stop the bleeding until we get to Rhode Island Hospital.

"Do you have anyone you can call?" He asks.

"I …have… a … husband Gregory"

"Does he have a last name?"

"Gregory Greyston."

"Oh, you're Gregg Greyston's wife? How did you manage to make it into that family?"

I can hear the sarcasm in his voice. I look at him in his rearview mirror.

"Since you know so much, Thomas made me pass the cut." I gave him a grin and he just turned his eyes back to the road.

We pull into the hospital's emergency room drop off and the cop gets out and goes inside. I tried to get out, but the doors were all locked so I had to wait. Finally he returns with a doctor in tow wheeling a chair over to the car. They help me out of the police car and onto the wheelchair, the doctor covers me up with the gown and wheels me back inside with the cop following on his heels. We take the elevator up to the second floor, there was an awkward silence in the air. I was relieved when the elevator door chimed and opened. I was wheeled over to the nurses' station to be checked in.

"Can I have your name please?" The nurse behind the desk asks.

"Gail Greyston."

The doctor who brought me up turns around and says. "Did you say Greyston?"

"Yeah?" I say puzzled.

"Ma'am your husband is here, give me a minute I will go get him."

I was tried to hide my frustration. I didn't want to see Gregg right now, I wasn't ready to face him but it was now or never. Thomas comes from around the corner, the cop who brought me in chuckles. I shoot a glance behind me and he stops laughing. Thomas looks so damn good in his jeans, timbs, and wife beater. His honey colored eyes fixed on me as he followed behind the doctor. I remembered why I was in love with him ,but my infatuation immediately turned sour when Quan came up behind him. The vomit rose in my throat and the doctor must of seen me binge, because he came with a trash can quickly.

"Gail what is going on? Why are you here? And with no shoes and no clothes?"

I say nothing; I don't have to explain anything to him.

"Sir? If I may" The cop interrupts the stare down between me and Thomas. "Sir we received a phone call about earlier that a woman was naked sitting on someone's porch on Taylor Street and upon my arrival, your wife was sleeping on the stairs and that's when I brought her here."

Somewhere between that cops story I felt myself nodding off.

"Mrs. Greyston are you alright?" I feel the drool slide down my cheek. "Let's get Mrs. Greyston into a room and bandage up her cut"

I jump up out my sleep like I heard something, and everyone is just staring at me. A young CNA comes sashaying her way over to us. I caught Thomas looking at her.

"Do you see something you like?" I hiss at him, he completely ignores me, so I go off. "YOU'RE THE REASON IM LIKE THIS! YOU FED ME THOSE DRUGS, YOU KILLED MY PARENTS! YOU MADE ME THIS WOMAN ALL FOR YOUR GREED, I HATE YOU THOMAS YOU RUINED MY LIFE!"

I'm screaming causing a scene. He slaps me right across my face, in front of everyone. I see the horror in some of the nurse's faces, but nobody says anything they all probably think I deserved it. He leans down and puts both of his hands on each side of my wheelchair He looks at me at eye level, his eyes were darker than usual.

"You listen here…I'm going to say this loud and clear bitch. What you did was your own choice. I never forced fed you crack, but that never stopped you from sucking on that glass pipe. Your legs don't look broken to me, you could have easily walked away and you didn't."

I put my eyes to the floor. Everything he said was right, I chose to stay and he never forced me. I was to blame.

"Shall we call Gregg bro?" It was Quan talking, I didn't even want to look at him.

"Take me to my room please." I say to the CNA and she wheels me away.

I hear Quan say. 0"Gregg we are still here at the hospital and a cop just brought Gail in. She's going to need some clothes." His voice fades off as I'm wheeled further and further away.

Gregg

Isaiah and I had been home about an hour when the phone rang. It was Quan informing me Gail had been brought into the emergency room escorted by a police. He didn't know much details, but he said she needed clothes. I was beyond disgusted but being a man of my vows, Gail was still my wife no matter how much I hatred I had towards her. Isaiah was sitting across from me when I got the phone call, I could sense the eagerness in his tone.

"What happen now pop?"

"Your mom's in the hospital, a cop escorted her there." I decided against telling him she was naked. I didn't need him painting anymore negative images of her in his mind.

"Do you think this has anything to do with her drug use?"

"I'm not sure it could play a factor, but I won't know until I get down there and see what's going on."

"Did you know she was using drugs?"

I was trying my best to give him honest answers "No I didn't son. There's been a lot of secrets in this house that I didn't know about."

"What secrets?"

I had to end this conversation fast. "Isaiah I need to get to the hospital and check on your mother" I rise from my recliner.

"I saw uncle Thomas slipping something to mom a few weeks ago." His words stopped me in my tracks. "Could he be the one helping her keep up with her addiction?"

Right under my nose my own brother was supplying my wife and in front of my kids, too many skeletons have fallen out of the closet today.

I ignore his question and asked. "Anything else you see?" My back is towards him.

"I saw mom give uncle Thomas money and he would give her small clear packages."

Well that explains how they ended up in our bedroom.

"It was a few weeks ago, they thought no one was upstairs but I saw them in the hallway, and then Uncle Thomas kissed her right on the mouth. I'm not stupid pops I knew something was going on."

" Isaiah I don't know what your mother and uncle Thomas have going on, but I don't want you to ever think your mother doesn't love you. Relationships go through hard times son and eventually all truths will come out."

"But why would she destroy our family? I thought when you take an oath in marriage, that it also meant being loyal to your partner."

"Yes son that is right, but your mother's drug addiction isn't allowing her to think correctly. I promise you son, this isn't how I planned out my family, but we just have to accept it and deal with it as it comes."

"The way you dealt with Grandma?"

We never talked about my mother in this house. "Isaiah, my mother destroyed our family…." I couldn't bring the words out. "Isaiah I have to go."

"Dad, I can take uncle Thomas out. He's destroying our family, feeding our mother those drugs. Who the fuck does he think he is?"

My heart grew heavy. I never wanted to hear any words like that come from my son or any of my kids mouth. I didn't want them experiencing the word hate and holding any ill feelings towards their mother, but it was happening and there really wasn't much I could do to change it. It was hard trying to paint a good picture of Gail to them when I loathe her my damn self.

"Isaiah there are other ways of dealing with these issues. Violence isn't the only solution."

"So what better solution would that be? Huh dad? We're supposed to just sit back and watch uncle T supply my mother with dick and drugs? As far as I'm concerned he is dead to me, but if you want to sit around waiting for a solution that's on you, in the meantime I'm going to personally have a man to man conversation with him."

I've never heard such anger and such strong words come from my son ever. I wanted to correct his foul language, but he needed to vent and I didn't try to stop him.

"Isaiah we really don't know what's going on."

"Dad are you serious? Do you need glasses? What, do you need for them to be right in your face? Mom isn't mom anymore, she don't care about us or our family. She been gone damn near two days and has not once checked on us, so what part am I missing?"

We hear the back door open then footsteps and our conversation comes to a halt. Its Elijah he comes into the kitchen where Isaiah and I were having this discussion.

"What's going on, where's mom?"

I look at Isaiah, he looks back at me. "I don't know Elijah we haven't heard from her." Isaiah gets up and storms out I call out to him "Isaiah!...Isaiah!" He kept on walking and the front door slams. I hear the car start up, I rush over to the door and step out on the front porch, but he's already reversing out of the driveway. I had no more energy to chase after him.

I had to get to the hospital and I needed to make sure my other two kids had someone to look after them, if I wasn't back in time. I never trusted anyone with my kids after what happen to Thomas. I buried that story with me for years. He cried out for help, but at the time I was caught up in my own life that I stop to see that his was being ruined. Thomas was troubled as a kid and my dad didn't want me getting involved with him. I regretted it every day and I wished that I had never turned my back on my brother. One of the neighbors agreed to keep an eye out and come over and check periodically for Elijah and Naomi.

"Elijah I need you to keep an eye out for your sister, stay close to the house and if the phone rings make sure you answer it, understand?"

"Yes dad, but where are you going? And when will you be back?"

"I'm going to find Isaiah" I told a partial lie. I was going to look for Isaiah, then after that I was going to find out about Gail at the hospital.

"What about mom?"

I couldn't tell him the truth I had already seen how sad my kids were before behind their mothers actions. I just couldn't take seeing them so disappointed again.

"She's ok, I'm just going to check on her." I hated lying to my kids, but I needed for Naomi and Elijah to not worry. Eventually, I would have to come to terms and sit down with them and explain thoroughly what's going on and answer any questions they may have. In the meantime I was going to get the facts. After reassuring my son that everything would be fine again, I left him with the neighbor's number and headed back to the south side to Rhode Island Hospital.

When I got to the hospital, I checked the time on my watch and saw that it was a little after nine. I drove slowly through the lot in search of a spot and found one that was right next to a gray charger. This was the same car that I had seen parked at Thomas house earlier. I jumped out of my car and walk over to the gray charger and read the license plate it was perfect match.

"Who better than Quan knew Thomas's address?" I thought out loud. It all made perfect sense. So not only was she having affair with my brother, but also with Quan too. My anger reached its peak and I felt like I wanted to hurt something…or someone. Who is this woman? I thought as I entered the hospital, I was so angry all I could see was red. At this point whoever I seen first was going to have a problem on their hands. I made my way over to the nurses' station and was about to ask one nurse about Gail, when I heard someone call my name. I turned around to see Dr. Stanford standing behind me.

"Hey Mr. Greyston, your back? Is everything ok?"

I'm confused of his questioning. "Yeah I'm here for my wife, Gail Greyston."

He had this worrisome expression. "Oh, well I hate to have to break the news to you Mr. Greyston, but your wife took off not too long. She took someone's clothing and shoes . One of the nurses informed me of this."

"What do you mean she's gone? How come no one saw her leaving?"

"Well Mr. Greyston, we have a lot of commotion going on in here and don't have enough eyes and ears everywhere. Your wife does have the option to refuse care."

"Where is my brother Thomas?"

"He's still here. I can take you down to his room if you would like."

I step aside and let him take the lead. We walk down the hall and make a right turn then walk some more until we come to Thomas' room. He informed me to ring the nurse bell if anything was needed and left me at Thomas' door. I entered the room as Thomas is walking out of the bathroom. I guess he didn't expect to see me back so soon. I spot Quan from the corner of my eye I went straight into attack mode. I rushed him into the medical supply cabinet and just start throwing blows at him. I didn't care if I was hitting his head or body, I just wanted him to hurt. Badly. My weight had him pinned between me and the cabinet, so he was only able to shield his face. So I turned my attention to his ribs and pounded my fist into them with much force. Then suddenly I felt someone grab me and pull me off of Quan, but I managed to break loose and start sending more blows to his face. He stopped fighting back after a while, but that didn't stop me. I grabbed hold of his neck and looked him straight in his eyes.

"Gregg!"

I punch him in his mouth and blood immediately spewed from his lips. The door to Thomas' room flew open and a few nurses and security guards came flooding in. One of the guards pull me off of Quan and moves me into one corner of the room. I looked down at my bloody knuckles and back over at Quan's bitch ass. Quan is just laying their unconscious and I didn't care.

In between breaths I say. "You fucked my wife." I break away from the guard holding me and run over to him and kicked him. "I could kill you right now motherfucker" I spit on him.

I finally come back to my senses of where I am and I look around for Thomas, he was no longer there. All the guards and nurses had a look of horror, but nobody made any sudden movements. I take one more look at Quan and walk out of there with his blood on my hands.

I was on a mission to find Thomas. I walked out of the hospital to the parking lot in search of my car. I heard a woman's heels clicking behind me, I stopped and turned around to see who it was, but no one was there. I found that to be pretty weird so I continued on to my car. when I got there I pulled my keys from my pocket to unlock the door. That's when I heard the clicking sound again, when I turned around to see who it was something hit me hard across the back of my head. That blow had me feeling dizzy as hell, I reached back to touch the spot where I was hit and saw my hand was covered in blood. I fell to my knees and saw a woman approaching me. She pointed a .9mm at my face.

"Well, well, well. Finally good to see you at your knees, you aren't so tough now, that little ass whooping you gave my brother was cute, but you know what's even better? Seeing you pleading for your life."

"What do you want Simone?"

"Your wife" said Simone.

"My wife? For what?"

"She owes my father a debt."

"Simone what are you talking about? What debt did my wife owe your father? I never heard any of this before now."

"OH! so you thought Gail was with you for love?" She burst out laughing.

That was a big mistake for her and a perfect opportunity for me to grab the gun from her hand. I snatch the gun from her hands so quickly she didn't know what had just happened. Before she could say or doing anything else I pistol whipped her and blood starts leaking from her head.

"Please Gregg don't." She pleaded as I pointed the gun at her. "Thomas sent me."

Thomas

Everything was crumbling right before my eyes. I had no idea how this was happening. Simone had been calling, but I wasn't answering because there was no money and she left me a message that she would be in town today. Gail's drug addiction had taking a turn for the worse and Gregg had found out that Gail and Quan had been sleeping together. I don't know how he had figured that out, but that was also a shock to me considering the fact I knew Quan was gay. He thought I didn't know, but I'm no dummy whenever there was pussy around he would turn his face up. It was confirmed when I heard the three way conversation between Quan and my boy Shaq's cousin Ricky, asking him to come over and put that naughty boy to sleep. I never met Ricky personally, so I wasn't fazed by the conversation. But I knew Quan pretty well and he didn't invite anyone to his house unless he completely trusted them. Hearing his voice on that phone conversation made me mad only because we been friends from the play yard and I never judged him and accepted him, but he still didn't have the decency to tell me himself. I felt the same way inside nobody ever stopped and asked me why I never had a girl, because they all assumed I was handsome and well put together I had all the bitches but I never had all the bitches. Money brings the women and women bring the headaches, but I had feelings for Quan. Which I found a little crazy because I despised gay men, blame my dad for that. All I ever wanted was to have money and respect like Mr. Blade, but nobody ever accepted me like Quan did. We both slept with Gail, which I had my reasons, but Quan I never seen that coming.

    I left the hospital in a hurry to find Gail because she didn't run from the hospital, I signed her out under Gregg's name. I found her clothes and shoes and told her to meet me at the abandoned house on Marlboro Avenue. I never seen Gail in such a bad state, but I was to blame for her addiction. She was my pawn to keep Simone quiet and she owed the debt to the Blade family. Simone contacted me yesterday saying if money wasn't in her account by today, which is a Tuesday, that she would personally kill me and my brother's family. I never meant to put Gregg into this, but for my cut of the money I needed to find a way to keep Gail all in and in close range, so who other than Gregg? He was an hour away at college and she attended the same college. I picked out her outfits and her style to catch his attention and I trained her how to act. Gail never declined she did as I asked. The only person not on board was my step dad, he sensed the fakeness, but I hushed him up putting overtime in on the block.

    Simone came into play when she came into her money after her dad's passing. Mr. Blade said she wasn't allowed to touch her trust fund and also explained about the debt owed. Out of the respect to her father the debt was to be paid in full and she felt like I wasn't living up to her father's expectations of me. It was starting to make me look bad and I needed to get to Gail. I'm weaving through the traffic from the hospital trying to make my way towards Marlboro. If I don't find Gail soon my empire will fall. Setting up shop on any part of the South Side will be shut down. I can't be labeled as the man not keeping up with my debts. I would soon be boss when Gail made these last payments and I planned on eliminating Simone once and for all. Quan betrayed me with my own bitch. Disloyalty can't happen on my team, I left his death to be on Greggs hands. I had a mission to focus on and that was Gail. I reached under my seat and pulled out my .9mm it was already locked and loaded and wrapped in a towel, I threw the towel in the back seat and place the strap on my lap. I pulled up to the abandoned building, tucked my gun in the back of my jeans and pulled my t-

THE FACADE

shirt over it. I got out the car and made my way toward the building.

Isaiah

I was on a hunt for my mother and uncle. I was riding up and down Prairie Avenue and Broad street with no luck of seeing any signs of them, but night time had fallen and that's when you catch everyone coming out. I'm seventeen and my mom decides this would be the best time to destroy our family and my uncle, that nigga's a bitch period.

I stopped by my boy Luke uncle shop in Washington Park, it looked like a normal car dealer shop across from the cemetery on the main strip. The owner we called "Papa" was also holding guns, you could cop anything you needed from him with no problems.

"Yo papa I need something nice and light enough to run with."

"Son you are too young to handle anything I got, so why don't you go play with your little friends" He laughed and I laughed when I snatched his pistol off his waist and pointed it at him.

"Do I look like I'm playing?" I pull out fifteen hundred and lay it on the table now get me what I need."

"Ok relax! I'll get you what you need."

I had found that money in my mom's underwear drawer, right along with the letter stating that me and Naomi were not Gregg's kids. I put the letter in her secret compartment she had in her bedside table, where I know Gregg would find it. I waited for Gregg to see it and tell me man to man, but he never did. He was a coward so I decided to take matters into my own hands, once I brought the blue steel .357 magnum with a pearl handle. I tucked it in my waist band like Simone had shown me.

Simone was my mom's old best friend, I never knew why they fell out and I never asked, but she made her way towards me when I was fifteen. She told me about the letter and uncle Thomas setting up the family. Once I found the letter I was convinced and uncle Thomas was a low down dirty snake who had to be dealt with. Simone made me a man. We never got intimate, but she taught me the drug trade and how to prepare, cook, cut weight and package the product. She taught me how to distribute the package too. I was the up and coming king of the south and my father (Thomas) never seen this coming. I just had to tie up these loose ends and end him.

    I saw my mother walking down Marlboro Avenue, she had on a small shirt and tight jeans bopping to nothing just talking to herself.

    "I'm gonna tear this up." She said referring to the package of crack she was staring down at in her hand. She never saw me park and got out of the car. She never heard me walking about behind her either. I knew she was heading into one the abandoned houses to get high. I quietly followed and watched her walk up the creaking steps onto the porch of one building. She opened the door like it was her home, there were no windows and no lights. I didn't get why she would leave our home for this. I see a gray charger pull up and I see my father get out. I duck beside the same building my mother went inside of and watch him.

"Son of a bitch.... he's dead!" I said to myself. It was now or never. I watched him enter the house and moments later I hear screams. It was my mother's voice so I pulled out my piece and rush inside.

<u>Gail</u>

Thomas convinced me to get out of the hospital, and meet him at the abandon house on Marlboro Avenue. He handed me a package of crack and sent me on my way. I was scared of what was yet to come. Would he hit me because I'm too far gone? I did as I was told and put on them little kid clothes and hauled ass to the nearest exit. I start running down Prairie Ave, Marlboro Avenue wasn't far. The crack Thomas gave me wasn't enough, so before I made it to the abandon house I make plans of my own.

A guy in a blue Honda Civic asked me if I needed a ride I didn't decline. I jumped in that white man's car.

"Where you headed pretty lady?"

I hadn't showered in days, my hair was looking crazy and he still found me pretty. I blushed and pushed my cracked lips up into a smile.

"I'm not going anywhere special, what would you like baby?" I rubbed his leg and licked my lips.

"What's your charge?"

"Flat rate is fifty dollars, whatever you want." I prayed it was just oral and that's all he wanted. I unzipped his pants and found his little penis. I felt bad for the man he was close in the size of a vienna sausage, he had no chance with woman. I chuckled a little, this would be a piece of cake. I wrapped my lips around his penis and five minutes later my job was done. He handed me fifty dollars and sent me on my way, I step out his car on Taylor Street and head towards Marlboro which was a two minutes away. I still hadn't eaten anything and I just was surviving off crack.

"I'm gonna tear this up." I was lucky I was still managing with no food, but this crack would fill my hunger pains. I walked into the abandon house and its dark and drafty, so I head to the bathroom where the only in the building worked. I pull out my crack pipe and lighter from my pants pocket and stuff it with crack. Just as I was about to place my lips around the pipe, something gripped my neck.

"PLEASE I CAN'T BREATHE!"

I screamed as the lighter and pipe I held in my hands fell to the floor. I was just about to inhale the white smoke that had begun to fill it, when I felt a pair of rough hands grip my neck and start to squeeze the life out of me. I scratched and clawed at the hands of this unknown person, as my eyes frantically darted around the room in hopes of spotting something I could use to fight back with. There was nothing in sight. I fought to breathe, as I felt my body gravitating towards the dirty shower in the bathroom that I was in. I had come there to feed my craving and was expecting to be floating on cloud nine soon after, but instead I was in here fighting for my life and I had no clue who the hands gripping my neck belonged to. I feel myself becoming light headed and all I could think about was how I'm here in this dirty broke down abandoned house that might possibly become my grave soon. Is this how I'm going to die? Did Thomas sell me out and was trying to get rid of me? Questions were flooding my mind as I struggled to breathe. Even in this fucked up situation, I wished that I was able to at least get my high before I died, that way I wouldn't feel a thing. My eyes suddenly felt heavier and it was becoming harder and harder to keep them open. Then out of nowhere something went *SNAP!*

    I fell into the tub with a big bang hitting my back against the soap holder built into the wall. I screamed in agony! I can't help myself and nobody can hear me. I stop screaming. I feel myself nodding off, my eyes are heavy and I see a figure standing over me, it was Thomas. I struggled to keep my eyes open and saw another figure approaching from behind him. Before I could form my lips to speak, darkness consumed me.

Quan

I woke up to the sound of beeping noises and I had an IV pumping fluid into me. I looked around the room and see that I'm in the hospital. The last thing I remembered was my fight with Gregg. My thoughts were interrupted when my room door opened.

"Day'Quan Robinson?"

I nodded.

"Welcome back"

It hurt to move. I realized I had a bandage on my head.

"DayQuan, do you know where you are?"

I respond dryly. "Yes I'm in a hospital." I look up at him for the first time and he was beautiful kind of reminded me of Gregg. He was my type.

"You got into a really bad fight. You got knocked unconscious. Do you remember what happen?"

I remembered getting my ass beat by Gregg, if that's what he meant. I was a battered gay man and Gregg was my abuser, once my body hit the medical supply cabinet I went unconscious. I didn't share that news with the doctor.

"Gregg did this to me?"

"I believe so DayQuan. You're one lucky fellow, considering the beating you took."

"What do you mean considering?"

"Well, after the beating you were bleeding severely, so we had to run test we check your blood. Your results for the blood work came back positive for HIV."

I look at him.

"DayQuan you don't look surprised by my news, something you want to share?"

"Who knows of these results?"

"No one besides myself and the staff who ran the lab tests."

"Ok good." I nodded.

"You know by law I am required to send this over to The Department of Health."

I pulled the covers back, pulled out my IV and asked where my clothes were.

"Where are you going DayQuan?"

"I need to get out of here, how much can I pay you to keep this quiet?"

"DayQuan I cannot accept money for silence it goes against my license as a Doctor. By law I have to report it and make sure you get the proper information and treatment."

"I don't need none of that."

"I understand that you don't want to deal with this, but I assure you that there are people who have been infected with this and were able to live long lives."

"Oh yeah? How so?"

"They seek immediate treatment after finding out about it. There medications available to help with the virus."

"So you mean to tell me I can live with this?" I asked out of curiosity.

"Absolutely." The doctor nodded. "But from here on out you would need to use protection."

Everything the doc was saying sort of sounded good, but I didn't have time for none of this shit right now. I had business I needed to take care of.

"How long have you known?" He asked.

"Let's just say I didn't ask for it to be this way."

"DayQuan I don't think anyone asks for this, but what you're doing is wrong and attempted murder if you're not telling your partners."

I get up from the bed and started dressing. I put on my sneakers and try walking past him, but he blocks my path.

"I can't let you do that DayQuan. You need to consider your options and actions. At this stage be fully aware your refusing treatment. Listen I took the liberty of ordering this prescription for you." He hands me a bottle of pills. The print on the bottle read Truvada.

"Just take these and follow the daily dosage. I would like for you to really consider getting proper care for yourself."

"I've taken care of myself enough." I shove him to the side and run out the door and down the corridor. I spot a waste basket and hurry over to it so I could throw the prescription in it. The I take off out the sliding doors. I had no clue where I was going, but away from the truth was better than anything.

I see a couple arguing as I run by. I see a man on his knees and a light skin woman in his face, I put my hoodie up and kept minding my own business. I start lightly jogging towards the direction of Lockwood, Thomas had my car and keys. My clothes had blood all over them and I lived in Pawtucket. My phone was dead and I couldn't call a taxi. I was pretty much shit out of luck, so I headed towards Comstock Avenue hoping that Thomas had stopped by there.

When I walked up all the little niggas were laughing and joking.

"What up?"

All laughing came to a halt and the lil' niggas looked me over with confusion. I'm on foot and blood is all over my clothes, this shit was probably looking crazy to them.

One asks "Yo, what's goodie my nigga? Fuck happen to you?"

I ignore any questions. "Thomas came through here?" I look at everyone all heads shake no.

"I thought I seen your charger on Marlboro." One of them told me.

I gave lil' dude a pound and walked away, I took Taylor street because it was the closest to Marlboro. Sure enough when I turn the corner my charger was sitting parked in front of an abandoned house. I put my face to the window and look inside, not a soul was in sight. I pull my hoodie sleeve over my hands and busted the window, it shattered to pieces. I looked around to see if anyone had heard or seen me, then I opened the door and popped the trunk. I walked around to the back of the car and dug around the trunk until I found the spare key that I had taped inside it. I shuffled around the mess in my trunk until I found an old shirt and used it to dust out the glass. After cleaning the seat of the car, I jump in my and take off. I had to relocate and chill out until things calmed down, but first I needed some dough. So I pulled back around on Comstock and told the lil' niggas to pay up. They all pay their weekly cut and I take off with no words. I jumped on I95, I wasn't sure where I was heading just yet, but seeing Southside in my rearview mirror made me smile. I was glad to being leaving this messed up place for a while.

Isaiah

I crept inside the house and its pitch dark. I had to let my eyes adjust to the darkness for a minute, then I made my way upstairs. There was little light emitting from one of the rooms. With my black hoody still on I peek around the corner into the bathroom and saw Thomas. I couldn't see my mom, but I could hear her. Thomas was just standing over her watching, as she cried for help any sudden movement I was taking my father's life. I pulled back around the dark corner and breathed gripping my gun tighter and just walked back into the bathroom with my gun pointed to Thomas head. My mom was alive I hear her say "Thomas watch out!" I looked down at her wondering why she was trying to warn a man who was trying to kill her. Thomas turned around and stopped when he saw that my gun was directly between his eyes. I looked in his eyes man to man silence was between us.

"What kind of father abandons his kids?" He looks at me and doesn't budge.

"You are not my son, but since you got that gun in my face you better use it motherfucker!"

I wrap my hands tighter around the handle of the gun and bite my bottom lip. "If you're not my father then who is, I saw the test results bitch!" I spat at him.

"You should ask your whore of a mother." He pointed in her direction and chuckled. My index finger finds the trigger and I let off three shots. Pop. Pop. POP!

Dr. Stanford

"Snap…snap…snap Thomas you can open your eyes now" Thomas blinks, "Do you remember where you are Thomas?" I say "Thomas?"

Thomas just blinks and mumbles what sounds like *He's guilty*. I have no idea what he means or what he is speaking of.

I was the psychologist at the Jane Brown Building where Thomas lived. It was a twenty four bed psychiatry inpatient facility located on the fourth floor of the Jane brown building, which was an extension to the Rhode Island Hospital. Thomas had been admitted roughly around 72 hours ago he had a lot of erratic behaviors that landed him in a locked facility where I , the psychologist give him an assessment to see if he's mentally competent for society.

"Thomas from my hypnosis and observation, I believe you are a paranoid schizophrenic. Do you know what I'm saying Thomas?"

He blinks and is mumbling as he's rocking back and forth in his gray sweat suit. "He's guilty. He's guilty. He's guilty. HE'S GUILTY!"

I just listened to Thomas repeat those words. I wished I knew what he meant by them, if he wasn't so far gone I could ask him. But he had no clue about anything, not even his whereabouts and he definitely wasn't ready to be released back out into society. I was going send out the letter to the state first thing Monday morning, stating Thomas's conditions and ask that he be a ward of the state.

"Thomas? Can you signal with your hands that you understand what I'm saying to you?" For a second he stops rocking. Then he goes right back into rocking. "Let me explain when I say paranoid schizophrenic, you are socially withdrawn, you have inabilities to distinguish between what's real and what's unreal, thinking clearly, managing emotions, and relating and adapting to your daily activities normally."

"HE'S GUILTY!"

I continue on. "My team and I think it would be in the best interest for you to stay here and get the treatment we have planned out for you. Thomas you could lead a healthy life with the right support, and attending groups, interacting socially and accepting the treatment. In order for the treatment to take effect, we need you to participate, communicate with the other psychologist who will be working with you, and healthy support from your family. Which so happens to be your brother, also a part of the treatment is taking your medications daily."

Thomas just continued to rock and mumble "He's Guilty!"

I stop talking and keep observing him, his hair was in a mini afro and he was growing a little beard, both of his hands are together like he's praying. He continues rocking and mumbling.

THE FACADE

"Thomas" I say "Have you understood everything I have said?" He continued to look out the window and kept rocking.

The Brother

After Thomas' bad break, they called me and told me they admitted him into the Jane Brown Mental Institution. I was advised not to visit until he was evaluated, now here it is three days later and I'm getting a phone call to come down so they can explain his condition. I thought it was for substance abuse, but the doctor said it's more extensive than that. I jump in my 2013 black Benz and make my way through traffic from North Main Street I turn up French Montana's 'I ain't worried about nothing' and bop my head smiling as I rapped along to the lyrics. My jewelry is glowing against my black Ralph Lauren polo. Heads were turning as I ride by, I was a nigga with money and style I loved the attention I was given for it.

  I make it to Eddy Street in six minutes and pull right into the parking lot facing the door. I jump out, lock the car up and start heading in. The sign on the door says ring the bell and look up at the camera, that's the only way you were allowed in the building. I did as the sign said and the door buzzed, the elevator was right there as soon as you walked in. So I pressed the up button, got on the elevator once it came down and pressed the button for the fourth floor. It chimed at the fourth floor I got off and walked up the small flight of stairs that brought me to double doors, it had to be opened by a staff member in all white.

"Hello, who are you here to see?"

I looked around the rooms at the pale green painted walls and got that hospital atmosphere feeling. I hated hospitals because it reeked of death and it gave the creeps. There were bars on the windows and I hear people screaming. Some were walking around in circles talking to themselves, I felt so uncomfortable.

"I'm here to see Dr. Stanford."

"Ok follow me right this way." I walked by the front desk and passed by, what were considered, bedrooms. The ugly shade of green didn't help the creepiness I felt. Thomas was not insight. The aide knocked on Dr. Stanford's door.

"Come in."

"Dr. Stanford you have a visitor." She said as she held the door open so he can get a view of me from his desk.

He takes off his glasses and stands and says, "Come in, come in."

The woman who walked me to his office just looked between us both as I passed her. Dr. Stanford fixed his crème colored tailored suit jacket.

"Carmen that will be all please shut my door on your way out."

I step aside and the door closes, we shake hands.

"Have a seat." He says pointing to all his chairs I take a seat in a leather loveseat. He walks from behind his desk with a folder in his hands and sits across from me. "Mr. Greyston, thank you for coming down on such short notice, but let's get down to why I called you in. Thomas has been admitted after all the testing and has been dignosed as a paranoid schizophrenic."

I sat back in the recliner straight faced. I was listening, but I said nothing.

"Mr. Greyston. I know this is difficult and not what you wanted to hear, but Thomas doesn't acknowledge that he's here. He doesn't participate in group and he doesn't talk to the therapist. All of this is from observation, his appetite has shifted and we started him on a medication called antipsychotics, which will help with his moods. We will continue with the medications, therapy, and groups on our end— but we need you to support as well. He will need all the help possible to get him back to a livable state of mind."

"Can I see him?"

"Sure I don't see why not, do you understand what I've said?"

"Just bring me to my brother."

We stand and I follow him towards the door, he opened it and allowed me to walk by him . His assistant, Carmen, was coming out of a room.

"Carmen where is Thomas Greyston?"

I looked at her and she wasn't attractive, but I pushed that out of my mind and waited for an answer.

"He's in the day room over by the window Dr. Stanford."

"Thank you Carmen."

We continue down the corridor I came up when I first arrived. We hit the corner and I see him sitting by the window rocking back and forth. He was due for a cut and new clothes, that gray sweat suit did nothing for him. Dr. Stanford stopped me before I approached him.

"You need to approach him by saying his name first, don't just walk up on him it could cause him to go into a rage and he can be combative. I'm going to leave you two to have some personal time to visit and to talk. If I don't see you when you leave you have a good day Mr. Greyston." He extends his hand and I give him my left to shake. Then he walks off.

    I put my focus back to Thomas, who is still rocking and watching the window.

    "Thomas?" The chair stops rocking, he looks in my direction it was like he could see right through me. I rub his left shoulder, he flinched and turned his head back towards the window and started mumbling. *He's guilty.* I grab a chair from a nearby table and sit across from him. I clear my throat.

    "How are you feeling?" I wait for a response, still nothing. "Thomas we need to talk, do you understand you'll be living here for a while?"

    Still nothing.

"Can you at least let me in on what you're thinking?" He continues rocking and looking out the window but he mumbles something different.

"Against me ... Against me ...Against me." I'm getting frustrated, but I know I have to be patient with him. He's rubbing his hands together, I touch them and he pulls back.

"I love you brother." I stand and just watch him stare out the window. I look out at what he's looking at it's my car he's staring at.

"Against me... Against me ... Against me." I bend down and grab him into a hug and he still continues to rock.

"Goodbye brother" I grab him even closer and whisper in his right ear. "I'm the king of the south now."

His body tenses up and I let go of our hug and walk off never looking back. I walked to the front desk to be buzzed out. As I passed by the nurse station I smiled at the nurse that is sitting behind it.

She smiles back at me and says. "You have a great day Isaiah."

"Likewise Gail" I chuckle a little as the door buzzes , once the door opened Thomas's screams started. I knew those all too well, he always screamed as a kid. I let the door close behind me and I hear banging on the door they are shaking from his fists.

"Its him…its him he took my spot." Thomas is screaming and banging on the door. I'm at the last step and I look back, I can see his eyes looking through the door windows and I flash him a smile and walk onto the elevator. His screams become faint. I pull my keys from pocket and walk outside. Standing by my driver side I see a man smiling with a brief case wearing a nice suit. I smile back.

"Well we waited for this moment Isaiah"

"Indeed we have Dr. Gregg Stanford" We shake hands and laugh.

"Isaiah?" Someone calls my name. I turn around and I'm faced with a gun pointed in my face.

"Did Doc over there tell you , don't fear the enemy that attack's you but the fake friend who hugs you" Quan lets off two shots.

ABOUT THE AUTHOR

Channel Walker is from Providence, Rhode Island she is a Certified Nursing Assistant and currently working on her next book.

You can find her :
Facebook:walkershantel@yahoo.com
Instagram:@chanelwrites_

CHANNEL WALKER

Made in the USA
Columbia, SC
30 April 2021